MISEDUC

Inequality, edi
the working classes

Diane Reay

P

First published in Great Britain in 2017 by

Policy Press
University of Bristol
1-9 Old Park Hill
Bristol
BS2 8BB
UK
t: +44 (0)117 954 5940
pp-info@bristol.ac.uk
www.policypress.co.uk

North America office:
Policy Press
c/o The University of Chicago Press
1427 East 60th Street
Chicago, IL 60637, USA
t: +1 773 702 7700
f: +1 773 702 9756
sales@press.uchicago.edu
www.press.uchicago.edu

British Library Cataloguing in Publication Data
A catalogue record for this book is available from the British Library.

Library of Congress Cataloging-in-Publication Data
A catalog record for this book has been requested.

ISBN 978-1-4473-3065-3 paperback
ISBN 978-1-4473-3066-0 ePub
ISBN 978-1-4473-3067-7 Mobi
ISBN 978-1-4473-3064-6 ePdf

Cover design by Lyn Davies
Printed and bound in Great Britain by TJ International, Padstow
Policy Press uses environmentally responsible print partners

This book is dedicated to Emily Smart, my grandmother and the most positive influence on my childhood. She defied poverty and a lack of education to become a lay Baptist preacher, despite being a cleaner and the wife of a coal miner. She cared about everyone she met, shared what little she had and never judged. It is also dedicated to my grandchildren, Scarlett Saitowitz, Max Saitowitz, and Cato Gokita-Reay. I write because of the past but also because, above all, I want you to live in a fair, socially just world where all children are loved, respected and able to develop their potential regardless of creed, race, class and gender.

What are the 21st century challenges shaping our lives today
and in the future? At this time of social, political, economic and
cultural disruption, this exciting series, published in association
with the British Sociological Association, brings pressing public
issues to the general reader, scholars and students. It offers
standpoints to shape public conversations and a powerful
platform for both scholarly and public debate, proposing better
ways of understanding, and living in, our world.

Series Editors: Les Back, Goldsmiths, Pam Cox, University of
Essex and Nasar Meer, University of Edinburgh

Forthcoming titles in this series:
Making sense of Brexit by Victor J. Seidler
Snobbery by David Morgan
What's wrong with work? by Lynne Pettinger
Money by Mary Mellor

Contents

About the author

Diane Reay grew up in a working-class coal-mining community before becoming an inner-city primary school teacher for 20 years. She is now Emeritus Professor of Education at the University of Cambridge and visiting Professor of Sociology at the London School of Economics and Political Science, with particular interests in social justice issues in education, and cultural analyses of social class, race and gender. She has researched extensively in the areas of social class, gender and ethnicity across primary, secondary and post-compulsory stages of education.

Acknowledgements

My thinking has benefited from the ideas and insights of many people. Firstly, the colleagues I have collaborated with on research projects over a period of 20 years: Louise Archer, Madeleine Arnot, Stephen Ball, Phoebe Bedell, Jackie Brine, John Clayton, Gill Crozier, Miriam David, Fiona Jamieson, Becky Francis, Val Hey, Sumi Hollingworth, David James, Cath Lambert, Carole Leathwood, Helen Lucey, Heidi Mirza, Caroline Oliver and Katya Williams.

I have also benefited greatly from conversations with Kathleen Lynch, Jessica Gerrard, Christy Kulz, Karin Doolan, Garth Stahl, David Pomeroy, Sophie Wee, Derron Wallace, Mona Jebril, Cora Xu, He Li, Lucy Howson, Birgland Magnúsdóttir, Jessie Abrahams and Sol Gamsu.

More specifically in relation to this book I owe a debt of gratitude to the two people who read my draft and gave me feedback. Les Back commented on my first full draft, while Julian Meteyard, as always, provided honest, unflinching reflections throughout the writing process.

The biggest debt though, as always, is to the parents and young people who gave so generously of their time and expertise. I hope I have done them justice.

List of figures and tables

Figures

Tables

List of abbreviations

BME	black and minority ethnic
DfE	Department for Education
FSM	free school meals
HESA	Higher Education Statistics Agency
NUT	National Union of Teachers
OECD	Organisation for Economic Co-operation and Development
PISA	Programme for International Student Assessment
SATs	standardised assessment tests

Introduction:
a personal reflection

Education and the Working Class[1] was one of the first sociology of education books that I read, and the first to have a lasting impact on me. When I read it I was an 18-year-old working-class girl, totally 'at sea' in higher education and failing to make sense of my own experience of social mobility at an elite university. There have been few books in my life that have elicited such a shock of recognition, but *Education and the Working Class* was one. Yet, it clearly was not describing my own working-class experience. Jackson and Marsden's text focused primarily on working-class students from families that constituted very specific fractions of the working class. They either were part of 'the sunken middle class' or came from the respectable, aspirant working class who limited their family size and saved up to buy their own home. Their politics were conservative, with both a small and a large 'C', and most of the young adults whom Jackson and Marsden interviewed lacked 'any radical impulses'. Rather, they were described by Jackson and Marsden as 'over-accommodating and emollient' as they struggled to fit in with a new, unfamiliar, middle-class milieu. In contrast, my working-class background provided a counterpoint to the many orthodox analyses of social mobility, including that of Jackson and Marsden. In my family it was not middle-class dispositions and attitudes that facilitated and enabled social mobility, but instead a strong, oppositional, working-class value system and political consciousness. I grew up on a sink council estate, the oldest of eight children, and was a free school meal (FSM) pupil throughout my school education. It is this complexity around the many different ways of embodying working-classness that I hope to capture in the text, and to further complicate through a strong engagement with differences of gender and ethnicity. It is important to recognise that I am also writing this book as a sociologist. This means that I understand social class in terms of relationships; not just economic relationships but, as referred to by Harriet Bradley,[2] a much broader web of social relationships, including those of life style, educational experiences and patterns of residence. As will become evident throughout the book, the lived experiences of the working classes whom I am trying to portray are also lived relationships both with their class 'others' as well as with those who share the same class.

I do not write specifically about methods and methodology in the book, although it is important to state that all my research participants have been given pseudonyms and the schools I refer to are anonymised. Most of the research projects I draw on are Economic and Social Research Council (ESRC)-funded projects and have detailed and thorough descriptions of research methods and methodology in their final reports, if readers are interested in more information. Yet, in the interests of personal integrity and honesty I feel that it is important to say something about my own passionate partiality. My working-class background influences everything I research and write. That passionate partiality is helpful in ensuring a strong focus on social justice and an empathic focus on working-class experience, but it can also result in an over-simplification of that experience that is particularly problematic at a period when class has become such a confusing, contradictory and slippery concept. It can also lead to a powerful sense of identification with a number of the children and young people whom I interview. While becoming an academic has involved a process of thinking against the person that class and community made me, at the same time there have always been powerful identifications in the field – strong desires for connection that trouble methodological imperatives for rigour. These are rarely to connect with those like the person I have become but, rather, with those very similar to the child I was – working class, troubled, difficult, out of place in schooling, a fighter but also a survivor.

My own memories of my educational experiences are like a series of intense intermittent flashes in the dark. They shine brightly on certain incidents, such as my first day at school, but flicker and fade in relation to much of the rest. They are also highly selective. I seem to have been primed to remember and hold on to all the petty humiliations and insults of class throughout my schooling. I can remember in vivid detail myriad 'put downs' and negative interactions, but the many days of quietly doing well educationally are a blur. In her book *Respectable: The Experience of Class*,[3] Lynsey Hanley recounts a much more balanced picture of good days at school occasionally interrupted by often-intangible class insults and slurs. But then both my immediate and my historical family seem to have had a habit of remembering the wounds and resulting scars of class. I grew up on my maternal grandparents' stories of the General Strike and the Great Depression. I was told that I should remember with pride that my grandfather was one of the very last miners to return to work in 1926, although he returned, bitter, bowed and his family in penury. In 1926, prior to the National Health Service, my mother contracted meningitis, and was in a coma for six weeks. She joined her older brother in hospital, he aged six and ill with tuberculosis. As a result, their grandmother, who was also in hospital with tuberculosis, had to go into the workhouse because my grandfather couldn't afford to pay the shilling a week that it cost to keep her in the hospital. He used to weep when he spoke of the shame this caused him. There was pride though, rather than shame, when he spoke of his own father's going to prison in 1927 for thumping the police constable who tried to take two rabbits from him that he had poached. Defiance, opposition and a passionate belief in socialism were the hallmarks of my childhood that I most wanted to hold on to. From primary school I was going to be a Labour MP, and can remember my dad pointing out George Brown, the MP of our neighbouring constituency, in a local pub. He had worked his way up, my dad told me. I might be a girl but I was clever, so if George Brown had managed to make MP so could I. But I didn't become a Labour MP, and the heroic, working-class stories that I was told, and in my turn retold, had very little to do with the everyday mundane realities of my working-class childhood, which were much more about squalor, overcrowding and adult depression. My mother had four children in four and three-quarter years, then a break of three years before having another four in rapid succession. As the oldest, I was never really a child, always an adult in making.

It seems to be the fate of the working classes to become heroes only of the past, never the present; and then, of course, those heroes are gendered, nearly always men, rarely women. I was astounded at university to be told by public school boys that I was lucky, even privileged, to come from such an iconic section of the working class. As a child I had been told I was scum, refused a place in the local Brownie pack because 'they didn't take children from the estate', informed by the girls at my grammar school that I lived in a slum and, when I ventured, with younger siblings and friends from our council estate onto a nearby private housing estate, told harshly 'to go back to where you have come from'. If someone had told me that my father was a hero I would have thought they were mad. What I most often saw was a defeated man whose work took everything out of him, leaving little for family or leisure. His life was one of night shifts, double shifts, fear of debt, frustration and exhaustion. His only source of respite was the allotment where he could dig the ground rather than toil under it, and escape both work and his ever-growing family. As Steph Lawler writes, 'narratives about working class people from both the Left and Right, frequently involve the past's reappearance as a positive counterpoint to the present'.[4] But I don't want to idealise my father's life; it was harsh and draining. The irony is that it was only in his late 50s, when he had a serious accident at the coal face, fracturing his skull and losing an eye, that he finally had time for leisure and other interests. Steph Lawler goes on to point out that today's working-class are seen as ignorant, stupid and universally racist. Yet, that is how I remember my family being viewed throughout the 1950s and 1960s. Owen Jones argues that since the mid-1960s the working classes have moved from being the salt of the earth to the scum of the earth, but if you were part of a large family and growing up on a council estate you were always scum.[5]

But, while the commonly held view of the working classes both then and now is that they are ignorant, stupid and racist, there were myriad class distinctions within the working classes, as well as between the working and middle classes, even in the 1950s and 1960s. For a long time I thought that being working class was about living on a council estate. I didn't realise that the foreman and deputies' children living in their privately owned terraced houses were working class too. But the working classes don't just include homeowners as well as council tenants, they encompass black and white, urban and rural, public as well as private sector workers, English-born alongside migrants. I only realised how atypical my working-class experiences were when I first read *Education and the Working Class* at university. It was only then that I fully appreciated that there were very many different ways of being working class, and I needed to be constantly alert to the dangers of generalising from my own particular experience.

But, over and above the difficulty of capturing much if any of the complexity of working-class relationships to education, there is a terror of getting it wrong. And the chances of getting it wrong intellectually are enormous for working-class girls. Yet, at the same time, the working-class relationship to education is what my whole life has been about. It shaped my tense and anxiety-filled schooling, and my later troubled experiences of university. It propelled 20 years of teaching working-class children in order to provide them with a better experience than my own, and drove an academic career in which the central project has always been one of understanding working-class experiences in education. In 1971, when I became an inner London teacher in charge of a class of 43 ethnically diverse, predominantly working-class, reception-aged children I thought I could provide them all with positive, enhancing educational experiences through the sheer force of my love, dedication and hard work. I was wrong. It was not enough, just as individual solutions are not enough now. I wanted to be in an educational system that supported my commitment to equality, but the Inner London Education Authority, one of the best and most progressive educational authorities in the history of state education, was never particularly good at tackling class inequalities. Over time, the conditions for the working-class children I was teaching worsened rather than improved. The developing culture of audit, regulation and assessment, the introduction of the National Curriculum, the growing reliance on ability setting, but above all the worsening economic conditions of the working classes, made the work of teachers like myself, who wanted all children to realise their potential, increasingly difficult and demoralising.

Throughout this book I try to use myself, or more accurately my own experiences, in order to sharpen my analytic lens. Some of my understandings of other individuals' class experiences are inevitably filtered through my own, but in ways that prioritise difference and diversity, and hopefully allow for insights that inevitably come from a shared class background, despite the differences of detail. But I also recognise, as Jackson and Marsden did, that we only scratch the surface. We can work only with the stories people tell us, and I recognise that much of the depth and meaning lies hidden in the pauses and silences. There is often far more that is significant in what people don't tell us than in what they do. So, inevitably this book is an incomplete and partial patchwork of narratives of class and education, a patchwork that owes as much to intuition and feeling as it does to scholarly rigour. The reason for many of the working-class stories in the book is not just that they exemplify key themes and issues – although they do – but that they also spoke to me in powerful and compelling ways. Just as Jackson and Marsden felt that their book succeeded in being 'coherent' and 'emotionally convincing … it explain[ed] what's going on',[6] so I want to achieve the best semblance of emotional truth that I, despite my passionate partiality, can.

The class landscape has changed enormously in the 60 years since Jackson and Marsden were writing and I was still a working-class schoolgirl. Then there seemed to be more certainties and fixity about class in England, and a general recognition that it told us something important about who we were and the society we lived in. Class and the many images that surrounded it were routinely used to place ourselves and others, not just in relation to the labour market but socially. It was a time when people knew their place. In contrast, there is now much more confusion about social class in contemporary English society, and people are less accurate when they are asked to assess their position in class terms. As Owen Jones points out,[7] it may be confusing to make sense of the changes in working-class composition from the working class of mines, steelworks and factories to one of supermarkets, call centres and offices; but thinking through class is still vital because it makes us confront the issue of who has wealth and power. It also focuses our attention on which stories and versions of the social world are listened to, and encourages us to ask why. Yet, while there is growing commentary on economic and social inequalities in England it rarely uses the language of social class. When it does, as it has post-Brexit, either it is in order to pathologise the working classes or else it is appropriated by one faction within the elite in order to attack another. Class is a zombie category. It is frequently buried as redundant, out of date, too crude and simplistic to tell us much about the complex society England has become. However, periodically, and with growing frequency in our current, austere 21st century, it rears its head, and there is a moral panic about class. Most notably within education this panic is about white, working-class boys falling behind, and then, post-Brexit, it is about the anger and resentments of the white working-class living in the Midlands and the North of England who voted disproportionately to leave the European Union.

Yet, there are still remnants, traces of a more proud working-class identity that exemplified the immediate post-Second World War years and the birth of the welfare state. Although working-class occupations are generally considered to amount to around just a quarter of the total, 60% of the British population define themselves as working class when asked to express a class identity.[8] So, a self-defined middle class is still a minority in English society. But, even more surprisingly, 47% of middle-class respondents in the 33rd British Social Attitudes Survey identified as working class,[9] so large numbers of professional people are claiming a working-class identity when they are objectively middle class. While not all of these had been socially mobile, a large percentage (61%) had been, but clearly felt they were still more working than middle class, despite experiencing a degree of educational and occupational success. This was double the number (30%) of Jackson and Marsden's successful working-class young people who still identified as working class. Of that 61%, 82% felt that the difference between classes was very or fairly wide, as compared to 70% of those who identified as middle class. The British Social Attitudes Survey report concluded that 'class identity, and especially working-class identity, is alive and well'.[10]

However, as I try to illustrate in later chapters, in the ways in which it haunts rather than animates political, policy and popular understandings social class feels more like the undead than the living. Furthermore, the strong retention of a working-class identity among many of the upwardly mobile shows just how powerful the pull of class loyalties can be. I discuss these issues further in Chapters Five and Six. This growing propensity to identify as working class in the absence of any strong sense of belonging to the labour movement is also evident in the US, once the archetypal middle-class society. While in a Gallop poll in 2000 only 33% of Americans identified as working class, by 2015 the percentage had risen to 48%.

This book is written out of a number of very different impulses. On the one hand, it is motivated by a passionate desire to provide evidence for and to support understandings of working-class experiences of education. But it is also born of a sadness, a need to make sense of and reflect on the damage inflicted on the working classes through education. The damage may now be very different in appearance and texture to that suffered by my generation, but its scale and intensity has not diminished. The way class works in education shifts and changes over time, but what do not change are the gross inequalities that are generated through its workings. It is also influenced by something that struck me very forcefully when I first read *Education and the Working Class* and still upsets me today. The conclusion that Jackson and Marsden come to when summing up how the majority felt about their working-class backgrounds was that 'most wish to forget'.[11] So this book is born out a desire to remember, however partial that may be.

The rest of the book

In Chapter One I discuss the myriad reasons why education cannot compensate for wider social and economic inequalities, drawing on both contemporary case studies and statistics. The chapter also compares and contrasts the more optimistic period that Jackson and Marsden were writing about with our current austere times. Chapter Two chronicles the history of class in education, starting with the introduction of state education for all in the 19th century. It moves on to discuss first the tripartite era and then the comprehensive school period, before examining the new, diversified state sector of academies, free schools, selective schools and comprehensives.

Chapter Three examines working-class educational experiences in the contemporary, diversified educational landscape. It draws on the narratives of working-class students and their parents to show the struggles of children to gain positive learning experiences within the English educational system, and the difficulties their parents often face in trying to support them.

Chapter Four explores in more depth the daily slights and humiliations many working-class children experience in school. It focuses on those children who are relegated to the bottom sets and those who are allocated to over-stretched, low-status, inner-city comprehensives.

Chapter Five takes a different direction in examining the experiences of the small minority of the working classes who are educationally successful. The first part of the chapter presents a different version of social mobility, one that uncovers the struggles and difficulties of the socially mobile, from Jackson and Marsden's working-class grammar school students to the working-class Bangladeshi young man I interviewed in 2015. The second part then examines the experiences of those working classes who go to university, and questions the extent to which a working-class student's degree holds the same value as that of an upper- or middle-class student.

Chapter Six moves on from working-class educational experiences to focus on the upper and middle classes. Arguing for the importance of seeing social class as relational, it examines upper- and middle-class educational practices and attitudes towards the working classes, and the impact of these for working-class experiences in education.

Chapter Seven focuses specifically on the emotional landscapes of class, describing how affective economies of identification and dis-identification are generated in and through schooling and higher education. Schools and universities are shown to be repositories of all kinds of fantasies, fears, anxieties, hopes and desires. While the greatest damage is inflicted on the working classes, the chapter also draws on data to reveal the damage inflicted on the middle classes.

In the concluding chapter, Chapter Eight, I explore continuities and transformations over time. What has changed since Jackson and Marsden, and what has remained the same? The chapter also looks at how and why the working classes fare so much worse than the upper and middle classes in education, and what we might do about this. Finally, the Epilogue provides me with an opportunity to briefly think through class and explain why I feel it is vital to understand the importance of social class in education.

ONE

Why can't education compensate for society?

Introduction

In 1970 Basil Bernstein wrote that 'education cannot compensate for society'.[1] This chapter argues that the main reason why is that we have an educational system that is enmeshed in, and increasingly driven by, the economy, rather than one that is capable of redressing economic inequalities. It is a system that both mirrors and reproduces the hierarchical class relationships in wider society. The chapter will draw on statistical data, showing, for example, the percentage of Gross Domestic Product (GDP) going to wages versus profits. It explores the relationships between the economy and education, with a focus on processes of privatisation and growing business influences, and asks how the working classes are constructed within a new, neoliberal status quo that valorises exchange value over use value and economistic ends over educational ones. It also looks back to the more optimistic period in which Jackson and Marsden were writing and compares and contrasts two very different economies and societies, alongside images and representations of the working classes both then and now.

In *Education and the Working Class* Jackson and Marsden argued:

> The educational system we need is one which accepts and develops the best qualities of working class living and brings these to meet our central culture. Such a system must partly be grown out of common living,

not merely imposed on it. But before this can begin, we must put completely aside any earlier attempts to select and reject in order to rear an elite.[2]

We are no nearer now to putting aside earlier attempts to select and reject in order to rear an elite than we were in the 1960s. In fact, in a period when the elite appear to be unassailable, it all seems even more difficult. Rather, our current political elite is engaged in a restructuring of the educational system, a retraditionalising of the curriculum and the reintroduction of policies, including the reintroduction of grammar schools, that work to mark out the working classes as educational losers.

A growing devaluation of the working classes in English society

This is not an easy time to write about the working classes, although perhaps there never was an easy time. Yet, the working classes of my youth and the working-class families in Jackson and Marsden's study had access to community resources, as well as to the support provided by social housing, the growth of comprehensive schooling and the new National Health Service, free to all on the basis of need. I grew up when there was a sense of hope and the beginnings of a feeling of entitlement.[3] The war had just ended, the welfare state was in its optimistic youth. Although there was a negative and deficit view of working-class culture it never quite reached the lows seen in the 1990s and since. There was a sense that the state was investing in the working classes and saw value in what they did and who they were. As Carolyn Steedman wrote about her own working-class childhood, 'being a child when the state was practically engaged in making children healthy and literate was a support against my own circumstances'.[4] An expanding welfare state and a pervasive rhetoric of providing services and homes fit for working-class war heroes in the two decades following the Second World War raised the sense of pride and entitlement among the working classes. It also softened some of the judgemental superiority of significant numbers of the middle and upper classes towards those whom they traditionally viewed as inferior. David Kynaston, writing of the 1950s, listed three occupations that symbolised the times. They were dockers, miners and car workers.[5] I and my family may have been called scum, but my father and many other working-class men were working in vibrant and thriving industries. There was hope. With hindsight, it has become clear that the 1950s, 1960s and early 1970s were a brief, positive surge in a more pessimistic current. The public sector has now, in 2017, been under threat for at least three decades. Class inequality has grown enormously since the 1950s. But the irony is that, in a society where social mobility has stalled, the working classes are often blamed for their own lack of advancement. They are presented either as 'decent and hardworking' – those who are engaged in trying to become middle class – or else as failures who are either not aspiring enough or not making sufficient effort to be viewed as successful individuals. Drawing a contrast between then and now, David Jones, a primary school head teacher from Bradford, in his evidence to the House of Commons Education Committee on underachievement in education by white working-class children, said:

> The impact of educational failure [in the past] was probably that you were condemned to a life of mass employment in whatever regional industry there was. Within that, you could be a fine, upstanding citizen and probably enjoy some of the cultural benefits of being in a brass band, working in textiles and all the other positive things that that working class life brought with it. Now, sometimes, it is to be condemned to the forgotten pile, and to have a life that has multiple deprivation and turbulence.[6]

As Jones makes clear, it is hard being working class in 21st-century England. The wages of the working classes have declined in real terms as a result of austerity measures, and their working conditions have become increasingly precarious as a result of the casualisation of work and zero-hours contracts. Half a million more children now live in absolute poverty than did in 2010, while child poverty more generally is predicted to rise sharply over the next few years.[7] In 2014/15, according to Department for Work and Pensions statistics, 28% of UK children were living in poverty, but the proportion could well rise to one third by 2020 if current austerity measures persist.[8] According to the Joseph Rowntree Foundation, 13.5 million people in the UK live in poverty – slightly over 20% of the total population.[9] Particularly worrying is the fact that the majority of people experiencing poverty are in working households, and the proportion has increased in recent decades.[10] This is perhaps unsurprising, given that the unemployment rate hit a new low of 4.8% in 2017.[11] We are being sold the myth of a country of strivers and skivers, but the strivers outnumber the so-called 'skivers' by more than 20 to 1, and it is they who, in increasing numbers, are living in poverty. We are seeing the running down of the welfare state, the erosion of universal benefits, a growing gap between the rich and the poor, the demonisation and undermining of trade unionism, the impoverishment of working-class workers and the reduction of affordable housing – in particular the selling off of council housing. The list goes on and on. Then, in 2016 the country voted for 'Brexit' delivering the working classes 'a double blow'. They were both blamed for the vote to leave and at the same time became the social group most adversely affected.

Increasing economic insecurity has been accompanied by growing political exclusion. Research shows that changes in the political system since the 1960s have increasingly marginalised the working classes.[12] And here, as in relation to the economic sphere, the working classes are blamed for their own marginalisation. Heath[13] asserts that the widespread belief that class has become less important in British politics is a false one. While it is certainly true that class divisions are not as evident as they once were, this is because working-class representation has been pushed outside the political system. In 1964, the time when Marsden and Jackson were carrying out their research and I was dreaming of becoming a Labour MP, over 37% of Labour MPs came from manual occupational backgrounds. By 2010 this had fallen to under 10%.[14] The promise of universal suffrage has been betrayed. Rather than the working-class being incorporated within the political system, since the 1960s they have become increasingly excluded from it.

It is difficult to untangle the many causes of the low standing of the working classes in English society. Does the growing lack of economic and political power drive increasing cultural contempt, or is it the other way around? What role does dominant ideology play in the process? How significant are a contemporary culture of competitive individualism and the dominance of an aspirational society in positioning the working classes as social and economic failures? On the one hand, what is the contribution of education to class relations in the wider economy and cultural representations of the working classes? On the other hand, how are economic relationships and cultural representations played out in the educational system? These are highly complex and contested questions that I cannot claim to answer. However, what is clear is the synergy between processes and practices in the economy and those in the educational system that work to position the working classes at the bottom of a hierarchy of value and respect in both spheres.

As a consequence, while economic and political circumstances change, the negativity with which the working-class are viewed does not. It is this historical legacy of being the inferior 'other' that resonates in the present. Deference always has been and still is expected of the working-class. In fact what is surprising is that some of the working-class still make enormous efforts to succeed educationally in an educational system that holds little prospect of a positive academic outcome. The working-class continue to have access to relatively low levels of the kind of material, cultural and psychological resources that aid educational success. Most cannot afford the private tuition and the enriching cultural activities that many upper- and middle-class parents routinely invest in for their children.

A 2013 study found that living in poverty corresponds to losing 14 points of IQ.[15] In contemporary, under-resourced state schooling the assets and resources that families can invest in their children's education both in the home and at school make the difference between success and failure. The new century has seen the advent of the 'scholarisation of childhood',[16] or what Annette Lareau in the US terms 'the concerted cultivation of children in middle class families'.[17] This is not simply an issue of material resources, the number of books, enrichment activities or private tuition sessions that middle- and upper-class parents can afford to pay for – and to which, conversely, working-class and poorer students lack access. It is also an issue of other, less visible gains and losses; on the one side, the benefits of affluence – confidence, entitlement, a sense of belonging within education that come with a family history of privilege, and on the other side, the consequences of families' histories of relative deprivation and school failure, which generate fragile, unconfident learner identities.

What becomes very clear in the case study of Josie, that I discuss in depth in Chapter Three, is that family histories going back one and sometimes two or three generations have a big impact on children's ability to succeed educationally. Working-class families do not have the same degree of confidence and sense of entitlement that the middle-class possess in their interactions with schooling; and so the negative representations and othering that characterised the past continue in the present. The lack of positive images of the working-class more generally contributes to their being disqualified and inadequately supported educationally. The following quote literally drips with disgust.

> As I passed The Boston Arms at the top of my road (a gigantic Tufnell Park boozer that has defied local gentrification for decades), I think 'Good God look at those pathetic old bastards hunched over their doorway cigarettes, their rheumy eyes, their stained darts shirts stretched over their cancered paunches, their broken veins, their pickled brains, their booze-emptied lives, heaving down red-hot, throat kippering smog as fast as they can and hobbling back goutily to the half-empty amber glass of misery they left on the sticky table under the telly'.[18]

Of course, not all the middle and upper classes feel the degree of class revulsion expressed by Giles Coren, and admittedly he is referring to only a specific section of the working class, but his words vividly illustrate that class disgust is alive and kicking. It is difficult to gauge how pervasive such attitudes are, but what is more certain is that they have contributed to a culture in which it is seen to be generally acceptable to scorn and rubbish the working classes. There has always been class derision. I remember in the late 1960s other university students laughing hysterically at Peter Cook's monologue on the coal miner and the judge in which he took the role of the coal miner. It went along the lines of:

> I could have been a Judge, but I never had the Latin for the judgin'. I never had it, so I'd had it, as far as being a judge was concerned ... I didn't have sufficient to get through the rigorous judging exams ... And so I managed to become a miner – a coal miner. I managed to get through the mining exams – they're not very rigorous. They only ask you one question. They say, 'Who are you?' And I got 75 per cent on that.[19]

I can't recall whether I worked out that we were being made fun of. But if you were and are working class, judging is always what others do. It is something that comes much more naturally to the middle and upper classes, with or without the Latin. But in 21st-century England the judgements feel harsher, more cruel.

The erosion of working-class employment rights in the labour market

It is partly this growing contempt, combined with the low value attached to the working classes, that has contributed to the erosion of workers' rights. Often, academics are personally detached from what is happening to working-class lives, but I come from a working-class family, and while I was writing this book one of my younger sisters, who has worked at a multinational supermarket for 17 years, was arrested and unjustly accused of collusion and theft of £45.95. She was held in a police cell for 11 hours while five policemen searched her house for evidence. They found none, but even so she was sacked for gross misconduct and left with no source of income and only the remote possibility of getting another job. But hers is just one of many examples of powerful employers riding roughshod over workers' rights. And there has been a stark and troubling erosion of workers' rights since the 1980s that has allowed their legal entitlement to diminish and their economic situation to deteriorate. The experience of being a working-class worker in the 21st century is increasingly one of exploitation. We are seeing an increased labour flexibility and casualisation that is particularly evident in the growth of zero-hours contracts.

Figure 1.1: Zero-hours contracts rate

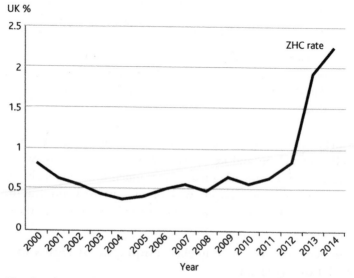

Note: Data shown are from Q4, 2014
Source: Labour Force Survey, ONS (2015)

The statistics in Figure 1.1 are for 2014. By 2016 zero-hours contracts had risen by 15% on the same period of 2014. They are symbolic of an increasingly insecure labour market in which the balance of power is tilted decisively in favour of employers as opposed to workers. Research by the Trades Union Congress (TUC) has shown that average weekly earnings for zero-hours workers are £188, as compared to £479 for permanent staff, and that two-fifths earn less than the £111 a week needed to qualify for statutory sick pay. As Larry Elliott concludes, 'This is not "flexibility": it is exploitation.'[20] However, zero-hours contracts are just the tip of an iceberg of deteriorating labour market conditions for the working classes.

The UK is becoming a low-pay economy in which the wage share relative to profit has fallen drastically (Figure 1.2). This, too, is a class issue. As the Resolution Foundation's analysis of the labour market shows, while only 1–2% of those in middle-class occupations could be considered low paid, the percentage in working-class occupations is much higher.[21] Seventeen per cent of those working in personal services are low paid, as are 23% of those in sales and customer services, and a staggering 34% of those employed in unskilled manual jobs. In 2016 Her Majesty's Revenue and Customs published a list of 198 employers who had been named and shamed for failing to pay staff the national living wage.[22] Among the employers were football clubs, hotels and care homes. The Resolution Foundation found that 'Only 12p of every pound of UK GDP goes to wages in the bottom half of earners, down 25 per cent in the last three decades'.[23] This is a global phenomenon, not just a UK one. On average 65–70% of households in the top 25 high-income economies

Figure 1.2: The falling wage share, UK, 1948–2011

Source: Lansley and Reed, 2013.

experienced stagnant or falling real incomes in the 10 years between 2005 and 2014.[24]

According to the Office for National Statistics, the median disposable income for the richest fifth of households in 2014/15 was 2.4 times higher than in 1977, once inflation and household composition were accounted for. The rate of growth of the median income of the poorest fifth of households has been slower (1.9 times higher in 2014/15 than in 1977). The Gini coefficient, which represents the income distribution of a nation's residents and is the most commonly used measure of inequality, is now higher than at any previous time since the mid-1980s.

The statistics are a brutal reminder of the low level of regard in which the working classes are held by those with the power to affect their lives economically; but the actual working conditions that lie beneath the statistics paint an even more shocking picture. A vivid example of how far workers' rights have been eroded in the UK is Sports Direct. Sports Direct is the largest sporting retailer in the UK, with approximately 465 stores. Its headquarters and warehouse are in Shirebrook, Derbyshire, where there are 200 permanent employees and over 3,000 agency workers. In 2016, the Parliamentary Committee for Business, Innovation and Skills concluded in its report on employment practices at Sports Direct that:

> Workers at Sports Direct were not being paid the national minimum wage, and were being penalised for matters such as taking a short break to drink water and for taking time off work when ill. Some say they were promised permanent contracts in exchange for sexual favours. Serious health and safety breaches also seem to have occurred.[25]

Workers were found to have 15 minutes' pay deducted if they clocked in just one minute late on arrival for work or on return from a break. The Sports Direct warehouse also operated a 'six strikes and you're out' policy. Under the rules, a strike could be given to a worker if they spent too long in the toilet or chatting, or if they took time off when they were ill or when their children were unwell. As the Committee concluded:

The 'six strikes and you're out' policy is used as a punitive measure, which denigrates the workers at Sports Direct and gives the management unreasonable and excessive powers to discipline or dismiss at will, reinforced by their power to control the hours offered to each worker. Workers are unlikely to challenge strike decisions, because they know if they do, they probably will not be offered any more hours in the future.[26]

The evidence to the Committee also revealed that these unreasonable working conditions were not limited to warehouse workers but also affected those working in Sports Direct shops. Seventy-nine per cent of Sports Direct store employees were also found to be employed on zero-hours contracts. The Committee described the experience of an individual working in a Sports Direct shop who was not offered a contract (of any sort), was bullied, pushed around and then summarily sacked with no explanation. The Committee's final assessment was that:

The way the business model at Sports Direct is operated, in both the warehouse at Shirebrook and in the shops across the country, involves treating workers as commodities rather than as human beings with rights, responsibilities and aspirations. The low-cost products for customers, and the profits generated for the shareholders, come at the cost of maintaining contractual terms and working conditions which fall way below acceptable standards in a modern, civilised economy. There is a risk that this model will become the norm.[27]

As the Committee goes on to point out, 'Although Sports Direct is a particularly bad example of a business that exploits its workers in order to maximise its profits, it is unlikely that it is the only organisation that operates in such a way.'[28]

The Committee's concerns about such practices being more widespread were confirmed by Steven Turner, Assistant General

Secretary of the Unite Union. In his oral evidence to the Committee, he said:

> This is a business model that we will find exported across not just retail and hospitality, the traditional areas where you find predominantly precarious work. This is now finding its way into transportation and logistics, supply chains and manufacturing industries. Wherever you find agency employment alongside zero-hours direct employment, you find the same sort of practices. One in five retail workers are employed on zero-hours contracts ... This is a business model that has exploitation at the very heart of it.[29]

This exploitative business model has already spread to the education sector. Foster reported the case of staff in a London academy whose teachers went on strike after the school announced its intention to introduce zero-hours contracts for staff. Time spent marking and planning lessons would go unpaid and teachers would be paid only during term time.[30]

In the next section I look at how being the losers in the economy has been accompanied by a lack of care and respect for the working classes within both wider society and the educational system. The section explores how their low value in the economy is mirrored firstly in the allocation of resources and policy directions within the educational system (discussed in detail in Chapter Two), and secondly in perceptions of, and attitudes to, the working classes in schooling.

From 'scum' to 'chavs': different words, same judgement

In 2004 the word 'chav' was Oxford University's first word of the year. Owen Jones, in his book *Chavs*, and Imogen Tyler, in a range of articles, have both written powerfully about the pernicious process of class labelling that culminates in the use of words like chav.[31] For Joe Bennett such words represent 'the flagrant triumphalism of the rich, who no longer challenged by those below them, instead point and laugh at them'.[32] If you enter 'chav' into the Mumsnet search engine you get over 3,000 results. Below are just a sample.

> Chavy as they come, kids have matted hair and are snotty, and the mums have greasy hair pulled into pony tails and look like if they could spell the word diet they would die of shock. I hate people like that. (Comment from 2011)

> Is Daniel a chav name these days? I ask as my husband keeps pointing out its often a chavkid name. (Comment from 2014)

> Mum 1: I was listening to Jeremy Vine on Radio 2 earlier. Jeremy asked in a totally serious tone, 'should the term not be used because it could be considered racist'. Unfortunately I was laughing so hard I missed the answer he was given so perhaps you could give me the answer. Could chavs be considered a race in themselves?
> Mum 2: Of course they are a race in themselves.
> Mum 3: I think you can be Black or Asian and be a chav. (Comment from 2015)

As Tracey Jensen concluded in her research into Mumsnet, it was primarily around the issue of social class that a whole range of dislikes and ill feelings emerged, including disgust, irritation and anger at different kinds of classed others, but particularly 'chav' mums.[33] The use of the term 'chav' underscores the representation of inequality in English society as being the result of personal choices. As Bennett points out, 'the word itself can be seen as related to a range of representations that serve in various ways to suggest that inequality (of both material and cultural resources) is to be explained by the deficiencies of the poor themselves'.[34]

This lack of valuing, contempt and class blaming found in the wider economy and society is evident in attitudes and 'beliefs' about the working classes in education. David Laws, the Minister for Schools at the time, giving evidence on underachievement in education by white working-class children to the House of Commons Education Committee, said that:

> Many of the problems with low attainment in school are due to factors outside the school gate: parental support, or lack of it; parental aspirations; poverty in the home environment; poor housing; and lack of experience of life.[35]

As I have already argued, many of the reasons for working-class underachievement lie beyond the school gate, and Laws does identify one of the key reasons when he mentions poor housing. But almost always when policy makers and politicians recognise that what happens outside schools has an even bigger impact on working-class achievement than what happens inside, they are citing deficit qualities of working-class parents – they lack aspiration, don't support their children enough, let them watch too much TV. So it is never about the wider economy, rarely about poverty and the lack of resources, and almost always about the working classes having the wrong attitudes and doing the wrong things.

The lack of valuing and respect for the working classes in wider society translates into class condescension and scorn in the classroom. Toby, a 12-year-old white, middle-class student at the Park School in the north-east of England, reveals how he has grown up to view the chavs as 'pathetic':

> *I take the mick out of chavs behind their back because I think it's just incredibly pathetic that you'd want to start a fight with someone really. [...] If they're going to be horrible [...] if they can't be bothered with school, um, it's just them that's going to end up being a dustbin man or working at the till at some sort of shop when they're older. So I just think of that and [...] just let it go.* (Toby, white, middle-class boy)

This lack of valuing and respect is also evident in the following quote from a London parent:

Plus, the other factor that goes into making the school actually good is (I don't know if it's particularly politically correct) but actually it is very low on the white trash factor you see. What you've actually got, is you've got people from all over the world basically and particularly you have got the Muslims, about half or a third of the intake or whatever. It has got much more of a tradition of education and like real fascist parents really (laughs) and so actually you don't get the same kind of disciplinary problems. You know they might be poor and they might be refugees but they have still got a very erm positive [attitude] towards the benefit of education as opposed to like the white trash families basically who are the third generation of Thatcher's dross or whatever. Actually if you get too many of those in the school then that is actually much worse than, people of different colour and races frankly. (James, white, middle-class parent)

James manages to insult both the minority ethnic and white working-class parents. But in his 'judging' he identifies a least some value in the minority ethnic parents that he fails to find in the white families.

There is also a troubling and stark representation of working-class low value and marginalisation in a growing number of schools that comes through classroom organisation and management strategies. The return of setting and streaming in primary schools can result in a very overt form of class labelling. It is difficult to handle emotionally when you are confronted with class groupings in which the lowest set of working-class, ethnic minority children are labelled the monkeys, while the predominantly white, middle-class top group are called the cheetahs. I discuss the impact of setting and streaming on working-class experiences of schooling in Chapter Three, but it is important to recognise the ways in which educational policies often work to reinforce and entrench the low esteem in which the working classes are held, rather than to modify and alleviate class prejudices and discriminations.

Conclusion

> There is so little that has happened in England since
> the 1980s that I have been happy about ... with
> ideology masquerading as pragmatism, profit is now
> the sole yardstick against which all our institutions
> must be measured, a policy that comes from false
> assumptions about human nature with greed and
> self-interest taken to be the only reliable attributes.[36]

Alan Bennett's poignant summation of the state of the nation
and the way all its institutions, including education, have come
to be governed by profit exposes the impotence of the education
system to solve wider social problems. Rather, as I hope to
show through the course of this book, it has become part of
the problem. Instead of enabling young people to critique the
society they are growing up in, on the contrary the English
educational system is enlisted in the manufacture of consent for
the elitist, deeply unequal status quo prevailing in English society.
Our contemporary educational system discourages free and
independent thought just as the board schools did 150 years ago.

One of the many important insights to come from Richard
Wilkinson and Kate Pickett's *The Spirit Level*[37] is that we
cannot divorce educational from wider inequalities. I have
briefly described these wider social, economic and political
inequalities. I have also touched on how the working classes's
decreasing economic and political power impact on working-
class experiences in contemporary England, firstly as workers in
the labour market and secondly as students in schools. Education
cannot compensate for society because our educational system
was never set up to do that, any more than it was established to
realise working-class educational potential. Instead it operates as
an enormous academic sieve, sorting out the educational winners
from the losers in a crude and often brutal process that prioritises
and rewards upper- and middle-class qualities and resources. In
the next chapter I concentrate specifically on the educational
system in order to focus on working-class relationships to
education, and hopefully to provide some clues from the history
of English education as to why social justice and equality are
still so far down the educational priority list. In analysing why

working-class children continue to be unsuccessful in education John Smyth argues that 'it seems that we have lost our way and headed down policy cul-de-sacs that have, if anything, manifestly worsened the problem by exacerbating educational and social inequality'.[38] As well as showing that inequality has always been at the centre of the educational system, I will examine a range of recent educational policies in order to assess the extent to which they have alleviated or exacerbated class inequalities in education.

TWO

The history of class in education

Introduction

> The function of schooling is to preserve the class and select the elite.[1]

In this chapter I present a brief historical overview of policy and practice before making a detailed attempt to answer the question 'What have been the historical processes whereby working-class educational failure has become legitimised and institutionalised?' Whereas the last chapter focused on the relationships between education and the wider economy and society, this chapter focuses on the workings of the educational system. I start with a concise overview of the history of working-class education in Britain before focusing on the recent history of class in education.

The history of working-class education in the UK is short and stark. It was only in the early 19th century that 'voluntary schools, mostly run and organised by the churches, became widespread. Even so, in 1818 only 7% of children were in day elementary schools, and shortly before the Education Act of 1870 was introduced still less than half of all primary aged children attended school.[2] It was only when voluntary schools were supplemented by a state-supported system after the Education Act of 1870 that a majority of primary school-aged children went to school. However, right from the beginning the class system dictated the nature and remit of schools. State-supported schools, or board schools as they came to be called, became the schools for the working classes, with a sharply different curriculum to those schools that served the middle and upper classes. As Margaret McMillan, writing at the beginning of the 20th century, makes clear:

> Was it possible that the children of the working class, however fortunate, however plucky, could hold their own later with those who in the formative years drank deep and long of every fountain of life? No. It's impossible. Below every strike, concealed behind legislation of every order, there is this fact – the higher nutrition of the favoured few as compared with the balked childhood of the majority. Nothing evens up this gross injustice.[3]

Andy Green, in his survey of the rise of education systems in England, France and the US, singles out England as the most blatant example of the use of schooling by a dominant class to secure control over subordinate groups. He maintains that the growing middle-class commitment to working-class education in the late 18th and early 19th centuries 'was different in every conceivable way from their ideals in middle-class education. Rather, it was a way of ensuring that the subordinate class would acquiesce in the middle classes' own class aspirations.'[4] From the conception of state-supported working-class education the system was designed to provide an inferior education, producing different educational opportunities appropriate to one's station in life. It was always about self-protection on the part of the upper and middle classes. They wanted to prevent any challenge to their own privileged positions, 'to inure the working classes to habits of obedience'.[5]

Adam Smith epitomised the English middle-class viewpoint regarding working-class education in *The Wealth of Nations* when he argued that:

> An instructed and intelligent people besides are always more decent and orderly than an ignorant one ... less apt to be misled into any wanton or unnecessary opposition to the measures of the government.[6]

For Smith, as well as the vast majority of politicians and intellectuals of the day, the schooling of the working classes was always to be subordinate and inferior to that of the upper and middle classes; a sop designed to contain and pacify rather than to educate and liberate. As David Giddies, MP, told the House of Commons on 13 July 1807, 'Education would teach them to despise their lot in life, instead of *making* them good ... it would render them *insolent* to their superiors.' Ashurst and Venn argue that one of the primary motivations driving the provision of schooling for the working classes was to remedy the 'disease of pauperism'.[7] As the Select Committee on the Poor Law Amendment Act of 1837 reported:

> Education is to be regarded as one of the most important means of eradicating the germs of pauperism from the rising generation, and of securing in the minds and in the morals of the people the best protection for the institutions of society.[8]

Writing about the introduction of state education for all 100 years after the publication of *The Wealth of Nations*, Jane Miller asserts that 'the provision of education for working–class children was thought of by and large instrumentally, rather than as likely to contribute to the life possibilities of the children themselves'.[9] When the English state schooling system was set up in the late 19th century the intention of the dominant classes was still to police and control the working classes rather than to educate them. Robert Lowe, writing in 1867, represented the views of the vast majority of the middle and upper classes when he argued:

> If the lower classes must now be educated ... they must be educated that they may appreciate and defer to a higher civilisation when they meet it.[10]

Then, as now, concern did not extend to a genuine interest in working–class education. Rather, poverty was constructed as an inherited condition that, if unmanaged, would escalate and threaten the social and moral fabric of society.[11] Also, the 1870 Act established an order that has never really been challenged since, despite all the subsequent legislation. What emerged from the Act were three parallel educational universes: elementary schooling for the working classes; secondary schooling for the middle classes; and private schools for the upper classes. The next sections of the chapter present a brief overview of how the educational system has evolved from its inception to the present day, the different forms that schooling has taken since the Second World War and how the challenges of working-class education have or have not been addressed.

Working-class education at the beginning of the 20th century

In the 1900s 5.3 million children were attending elementary schools but only 172,000 of them were going on to secondary schooling.[12] By 1913 only 5.8% of 14- to 16-year-olds were in secondary education. Throughout this period it is clear that legislation and actual educational practice were two different things. It was one thing to make schooling compulsory up to 14 years of age, but it was a very different thing to make it possible for working-class children to attend. Throughout the 1920s there were still only 7% of children aged 11 to 15 attending state secondary schools. My father and all his eight siblings stopped attending school in the late 1920s and 1930s when they reached the age of 11 or 12, to take on unskilled labouring work. Their father's ill health and early death meant that they all had to start earning money as soon as possible. And by the late 1930s still only 10% of elementary school pupils were moving on to secondary schools. The rest either remained in 'all-age' schools or went on to senior schools, leaving at 13 or 14 or even earlier. The working classes were still receiving a totally different education to the upper and middle classes. If they wanted to stay on and move into a secondary school they were often expected to contribute financially. It was not until the Education Act of 1944 that fees were finally prohibited in state secondary schooling. Throughout the first half of the 20th century the working classes were not receiving a different but parallel education to the middle and upper classes, they were receiving considerably less education that often ended when they reached adolescence. This was all to change with the introduction of the tripartite system, which I discuss in the next section.

The grammar school and the failure of the tripartite system

> One of the greatest paradoxes of what is called the 'democratization of schooling' is that only when the working classes, who had previously ignored or at best vaguely concurred in the ideology of 'schooling as a liberatory force' ... actually entered secondary education, did they discover ... schooling as a conservative force, by being relegated to second-class courses or eliminated.[13]

The establishment in 1944 of a tripartite system of education came with the renewed promise of tackling working-class underachievement through an exam at age 11 to select the 'brightest' children on the basis of ability. Those pupils who passed the 11-plus got into a grammar school; the rest went into non-selective secondary moderns; and there was also a technical college strand, although very few such colleges were ever built. The rhetoric was that grammar schools were to take the 25% most academically able children, regardless of class background, and to substantially increase educationally opportunities. The reality was very different, as Halsey, Heath and Ridge found in their research, which spanned the 1930s to the 1970s and assessed the progress made by grammar schools up to 1972.[14] They concluded that 'school inequalities of opportunity have been remarkably stable over the forty years which our study covers. Throughout, the service class has had roughly three times the chance of the working class of getting some kind of selective secondary schooling.'[15] Even those working-class children who did get into grammar schools were frequently relegated to the bottom sets on the basis of their 'ability'. As Julienne Ford found in her research in three London secondary schools (a grammar school, a secondary modern and a comprehensive), '46 per cent of the middle class children in the grammar school with high IQs were placed in the A stream, while only 10 per cent of the working class children in the same ability range achieved that placement'.[16] The Mary Evans quote later in the chapter, and my own experience, reinforce Ford's finding that top sets were largely working-class-free zones. After I moved into the top set at the end of my first year at grammar school I was never in a class with more than one other working-class girl.

The wider evidence on grammar schools as potential vehicles for working-class social mobility seems to reinforce my own personal experiences. Douglas et al, in their survey of 5,362 secondary school pupils, discovered that for those pupils who went to grammar school there was a change in attainment, which resulted in the clustering of the middle-class children towards the upper end of each year, while the working-class students were grouped towards the lower end.[17] They found over the four years of their study that the social classes, who had been slightly apart in their reading scores but equivalent in terms of maths scores, 'moved apart in both the attainment tests'.[18]

The appointment in 2016 of a new Conservative Prime Minister, Theresa May, brought with it the reassertion of the same old educational myth – that more grammar schools would address working-class underachievement and raise social mobility. In her speech on 9 September 2016 she claimed that her vision was for a truly meritocratic Britain that put the interests of ordinary, working-class people first. For May, the main means of achieving this were to be grammar schools, and she went on to argue:

> Grammar schools are hugely popular with parents. We know they are good for the pupils that attend them. Indeed, the attainment gap between rich and poor pupils is reduced to almost zero for children in selective schools. And we know that they want to expand. They provide a stretching education for the most academically able, regardless of their background, and they deliver outstanding results.[19]

Yet, current research analysing the government's proposals found that for a child to have even a 50–50 chance of getting into one of May's new grammar schools they would need to be in one of the wealthiest 10% of families in the country.[20] And the few working-class children who do beat the odds rarely shine academically. When grammar schools deliver outstanding results these are nearly always for middle-class children. The statistics show that in the 1960s, although working-class pupils made up 26% of grammar school pupils, children from unskilled, manual working-class backgrounds represented only 0.3% of those who achieved two A-Levels or more.[21] In 1963 the Robbins Report found that 33% of those whose fathers were higher professionals went on to get degrees, while only 2% of those from skilled working-class backgrounds, and just 1% of those from semi- or unskilled backgrounds, did so.[22] In the 1950s two-thirds of children from unskilled working-class backgrounds left grammar school with less than three O-Levels.[23] Douglas et al's conclusion is equally depressing. They expressed regret that:

> It was to be expected that nearly all the pupils of high ability, some of whom had struggled against considerable difficulties to reach the grammar schools, would be supported by the academic traditions of their schools and stay on at least to enter the sixth form. This was not so and it is disturbing to find so many leave early and fail to sit the General Certificate examinations.[24]

They found that the 'lower manual working class displayed the greatest waste of talent'. Jackson and Marsden wrote that the working-class children in their sample who made it to grammar school came from 'the very upper reaches of the working class',[25] which is perhaps why they were, on balance, more successful than Douglas et al's much larger sample. But even so, many experienced insecurity, uncertainty and confusion. They lost any sense of belonging, with a number talking about feeling as if they were 'in a haze', perplexed by the strangeness and sheer difference of their new school. There are echoes of similar estrangement in Valerie Walkerdine's poignant reflection that entering grammar school in 1958 'meant for years I would no longer feel any sense of belonging, nor any sense of safety'.[26] My uncle, who lived on the same council estate that I grew up on, was slightly older than both Walkerdine and Jackson and Marsden's working-class grammar school pupils. He had a brutal, uncompromising view of his time in a boys' grammar school in the mid-1950s. He wrote a poem about what he saw as the systematic persecution of boys from the local council estate:

> 'Northfield boys all in a line' So went the chilling command,
>> Staccato-fired as a bullet, aimed at a very small band
>> Of some at the grammar school
>> Who were not really welcome at all
>
> The town was pretty and proud, the inhabitants mostly well heeled,
>> Though the lads from the council estate, built on the northern fields
>> They came from the poorest class,
>> The headmaster's chosen outcasts
>> His cane was supple and thin, designed to inflame the skin
>> The punishment short and sore, the boys determined to stand
>> Showing no sign of fear
>> Shedding never a tear
>
> They called it Jackson's school, for Jackson was his name
>> He ruled with a rod of iron and whenever a problem came
>> Be it vandalism or noise
>> He blamed the Northfield boys.

Although he managed to get into the higher sets and left at the age of 16 with reasonable qualifications, my uncle hated his grammar school. He saw his secondary schooling as a process of attrition, a wearing down and wasting of the working classes, and in particular those from the council estate whom Jackson, the head teacher, saw as rough and undeserving. However, the most graphic description of the grammar school as the preserve of the middle classes, and the consequences for the small number of working-class who struggled over the barricades, can be found in Mary Evans' autobiographical account of her 1950s grammar schooling. She wrote:

> Unless middle-class children could not do the most simple mathematics I suspect the 11-plus was impossible to fail – or to put it another way the 11-plus was almost impossible for working-class children to pass. So those of us selected were extremely homogenous. Arriving at grammar school on the first day of the first term, the most striking characteristic of the other new pupils was that they too arrived in cars, from detached homes and with standard English voices. Nevertheless, one or two working-class pupils did enter this select and selected world. Yet, how they were expected to survive and not commit suicide in the playground is a vivid if retrospective question. Two practices of the school made class divisions and distinctions immediately apparent. During the first week we all had to complete forms giving our father's occupation and submit to a shoe inspection. The exercise of completing the form about our personal circumstances revealed the inevitable parade of middle-class occupations, as doctors followed architect, solicitor, bank manager, teacher, civil servant, university lecturer and so endlessly on and on, it was really bad luck, almost bad form, to interrupt this panorama of suburban life with a lone voice saying factory worker or merchant seaman. Those two occupations struck me at the time as part of a foreign and bizarre world.[27]

For most working-class grammar school pupils, attending a grammar school was not a particularly positive experience. Unlike the majority of Jackson and Marsden's sample, who ended up in the top stream, most found themselves struggling in the bottom streams. But the greatest damage inflicted by the grammar schools was not on those few working classes who gained entry but on the far larger group of working-class children who failed the 11-plus and ended up in secondary modern schools. As Michael Young wrote, 'Every selection of one is a rejection of many.'[28]

Secondary moderns were secondary in more than one way. They were seen as second-rate provision for less-intelligent children and, as such, were subject to poor funding and a narrow curriculum. In 1950s it was estimated that the average grammar school pupil received 170% more per annum, in terms of resources, than the average secondary modern school child. But there were class differences within secondary modern schools. Douglas et al found in their 1971 study that there were a higher percentage of middle-class children in the better-staffed and better-resourced secondary moderns, whereas working-class children were more often to be found in secondary modern schools with poor buildings, and where staff shortages were frequently reported.[29] The limitations of a secondary modern curriculum were evident in this statement made to the House of Commons in 1956:

> Secondary modern schools, like all schools, are social institutions as well as places of instruction. Literacy and mastery of the 'three Rs' must be accompanied by a respect for hard work, self-discipline and good manners. They are concerned as well to give to the duller children a sense of competence and achievement, to the average all-round development of their brains and bodies, to the brightest a challenge to stretch themselves.[30]

Heaton, a secondary modern head teacher in the 1950s, described the harsh effects of selection in his own school, observing the inbuilt sense of failure and alienation experienced by many of his pupils. He reflected that: 'Almost the first words uttered by the parents of a new boy in 1950 were "I want him to have another chance for the scholarship"' while for most pupils the main objective was to leave school as quickly as possible.

He went on to argue:

They are the schools which have been subjected to more calumny and vilification than any other type of school ever evolved in these islands. The use of the term 'Secondary' to denote 'second stage' in 1944 misled many of the general public into the illusion that somehow 'Secondary Education for All' meant 'Grammar School Education for All'. This was not so, and because of the disillusionment which followed the secondary modern schools bore the brunt of the attack which came from all quarters.[31]

In contrast to the many 'heroic' tales of working-class-made-good grammar school pupils, the many more working-class individuals who went to secondary modern schools were understandably less keen to write about their experiences. Jackson and Marsden did not look at the experience of working-class children in secondary modern schools but, while their working-class children were having a difficult time in grammar schools, their secondary modern peers were experiencing a sense of failure and rejection that was far worse. As Elvis Costello sang about his own experience of going to a secondary modern in the 1970s:

This must be the place
Second place in the human race
Down in the basement.

As one anonymous 11-plus failure wrote in the *Guardian* in 2015 'going to a secondary modern school full of people who were "failures" was not a positive experience'. The writer argued that labelling thousands of children in this way and putting them in a school together was clearly a recipe for failure, maintaining that to be written off as a 'failure' at age 10 or 11 was a travesty. They argued that achieving any sense of educational success had been a battle, and concluded that the effects of failure were deep rooted and continued to impact on them more than 30 years later. More recently, Chris Horrie has written an extended essay on his own secondary modern school experience in the 1960s. He explained that only three subject areas were taken seriously by the school:

Religious education, woodwork for boys and domestic science for girls. Metalwork seemed to disappear from the curriculum after the tough kids turned the lathe area into a weapons factory, manufacturing a steady stream of improvised but deadly-looking crossbows. Girls were not allowed to do woodwork because it was too dangerous and 'unladylike'. Instead they had a specially arranged workshop set out like a kitchen with rows of ironing boards, where they could practise doing things such as washing dishes and ironing clothes.[32]

Horrie goes on to describe how many of his fellow students were crushed by the experience of failing the 11-plus, asserting that most of the young people he was at school with were at least as intelligent as him, and many were brilliant. He considered that some were probably dyslexic, before the condition was really recognised. He concludes, 'Few of them went on to higher education. Who will speak for them?'

Ironically, the most potent political impetus for change came from a concern to address not the appalling amount of working-class underachievement caused by the tripartite system but, rather, the growing anger and outrage of disenfranchised middle-class parents whose children had failed to get into grammar schools.[33] From the 1960s onwards both central government and local authorities began to prefer all-ability comprehensive schools as a way of providing a better education to the 75% of children forced into inadequate secondary moderns. The newly elected Labour government of 1964 came to power with a manifesto that included the creation of a comprehensive system of education.

Comprehensive schooling and missed opportunities

The system will increasingly ... be built around the comprehensive school....All schools will more and more be socially mixed; all will provide routes to the Universities and to every type of occupation from the highest to the lowest.... Then very slowly, Britain will cease to be the most class-ridden country in the world.[34]

Comprehensive schooling was to address the tripartite system's failure to harness working-class educational potential. However, right from the beginning comprehensive reform in England was implemented in a very uneven way. According to Jones, it lived in the shadow of selective education and in many cases perpetuated selective arrangements.[35] Although the wider unequal class structure does not define comprehensive schooling in the way it did the tripartite system, social class inequality remained a key feature of the system. It was evident in children's informal associations at school, as 'comprehensive schooling failed to neutralise the impact of class background on children's friendship patterns'.[36] But it was also built into the formal structures of the comprehensive school. Selection through the 11-plus examination was replaced in many comprehensives by selection through streaming. This too was a process of social class selection. As Bob Burgess vividly describes in relation to the comprehensive school he researched:

> Separate sets of expectations were built up that led to the development of an alternative form of schooling within the school, in such a way that the label 'comprehensive' merely covered a number of activities that took place on one site.[37]

These different educational expectations were expressed through systems of setting and streaming. And, as I describe in more detail in Chapter Four, it was primarily working-class children who were placed in the bottom sets, while middle-class children clustered in the top sets. But the greatest problem lay outside the school gates, in the patterns of residential segregation that determined comprehensive school intake. Many comprehensive schools were neighbourhood schools, catering for children from a limited catchment area, and many such areas were occupied predominantly by one social class or another. As a consequence, even from the outset, some comprehensives could be described as working class, and others as middle class. All this added up to a new comprehensive educational system that, like the tripartite system, mirrored wider social inequalities rather than compensating for them. As a result, although comprehensive schooling did not replicate the deep social class divides caused by the 11-plus, it has never fulfilled the promises of its early advocates. This was starkly revealed in Benn and Chitty's research on the educational outcomes of comprehensive schools by the social class composition of their intakes.[38] In 1994, of their sample of 1,542 schools, predominantly working-class comprehensives were achieving 26% five or more GCSE grades A–C, while predominantly middle-class schools were achieving 55%. They found that highly class-polarised comprehensives made up a third of their sample, while the class-balanced comprehensives were a much smaller percentage at 13%. However, the results for this much smaller group of schools with a fairly equal working- and middle-class intake were higher than expected at 47%, and Benn and Chitty argue that social mixing 'might produce its own positive effect'. However, there was never the political will or sufficient policy emphasis to put Benn and Chitty's suggestion to the test. Around the same time that Benn and Chitty were doing their research parallel research by Gewirtz, Ball and Bowe found what they called 'a decomprehensivisation' of secondary schools. They argued that:

> working class children are on the whole likely to be ghettoized in under-subscribed, understaffed, low-status schools. At the same time middle-class parents are most likely to apply and have their children selected for the oversubscribed, favourably resourced, favourably staffed, high status schools.[39]

This is still true over 20 years later. In fact, since the 1990s the growing emphasis on parental choice and market forces has led to more polarisation and less-balanced intakes. Jackson and Marsden's prescient comment that comprehensives would enclose grammar schools rather than abolishing them needs to be extended to secondary modern schools too. While the tripartite system segregated social classes in different school buildings, the comprehensive system segregates them within the same school building. This was recognised by many of the parents in my ESRC project on the white middle classes sending their children to diverse urban comprehensives. As one mother explained, her initial concerns about poor behaviour and ill discipline had been ill founded because her daughter's comprehensive 'is very much like two schools in that, you know, if you're in the top sets you're in one school, it's a bit like grammar and secondary modern all in one school'.

We have never had a fair educational system. But now, in the 21st century, we are seeing the dissolution of a comprehensive system that was never fully comprehensive even at the outset, and its replacement by new elements that combine selection, elitism and patronage under the guise of providing diversity and choice. The features of this model are evident in the implementation of intensive testing, the widening range of selective and specialist schools, the focus on meeting the needs of gifted and talented children and the policy obsession with aspiration and opportunity.[40] As Stephen Ball argues, as far as social inequality is concerned, education policy is not working, or not working very well.[41] The class gap in attainment is wide and widening. In 2015 the educational achievement gap between working- and middle-class pupils widened for the first time in recent years, as exam results showed that just one in three lower-income students reached the government's GCSE pass target, compared with more than 60% of middle-class students.[42] After much time, effort and career building by academics focusing on how to improve the effectiveness of schools, the consensus currently is that schools account for between 5% and 50% of the class differences in attainment. So, in order to address and reduce at least half of this class difference we need to look beyond the school gates rather than within them. There is only so much that educational institutions can do to improve social class inequalities, given the economic and social context in which they operate. As Ball concludes, schools are increasingly the wrong place to look if we want to do something about class inequalities in education. But I am not suggesting that policy changes are not important. They are crucial if we are to enhance working-class children's educational experiences and give children a sense of well-being and belonging in schooling. One of the most insightful reflections on the state of education in the modern period, which is even more true today, was Phil Brown's assertion in 1990 that 'a child's education is increasingly dependent on the wealth and wishes of parents, rather than the ability and efforts of pupils'.[43] But while the balance between wealth and wishes and ability and effort has been shifting towards the former within the state sector, for the upper classes education has always been predicated on their wealth and desires for exclusivity.

Private schooling: ideal, or nemesis of the state sector?

Our state educational system is a class-polarised, one but the archetypal model of class-segregated education is the private school system with its intertwining of classism with sexism. The history of private schooling has always been a history of elitism and, for the most part, it has also been a history of boys' education. When we look at Jackson and Marsden's insights from over 60 years ago it rapidly becomes apparent that the socially just educational system they were promoting would require a very different structure to the existing one, with a much flatter hierarchy of schooling; but first and foremost it required the abolition of the private schools. Bourdieu wrote of the grandes écoles in France as 'enclosures separated from the world, quasi-monastic spaces where they live a life apart, a retreat, withdrawn from the world and entirely taken up with preparing for the most "senior positions"'.[44] But the description applies equally well to the elite private schools in England, which functioned and still function as England's 'schools of power'.[45] Currently at least 18% of English school educational spending goes on the 7% of pupils who are privately educated.[46] We spend more on our private school system than does any other country except Chile. But over and above such an inequitable distribution of resources, private schools have been one of the principal means by which elitism and social divisions are produced and perpetuated in England. The faltering commitment to comprehensive schooling is fundamentally undermined by structures, such as private schools, that perpetuate advantage and segregated schooling. Jackson and Marsden were quite clear that scholarships for the working classes in private schools were not a solution. Rather, they argued that partnership between private and state schools would just put 'the same people in the same places at the same price'.[47]

But the private schools are not just about elitism and exclusivity. They are also the chief means through which the upper classes operate a form of monopoly privilege, enabling them to ring-fence high-status positions across all areas of the economy. These include politics, the law, finance and the media, but also acting and sport.[48] In 2016, the proportion of privately educated British sports people taking part in the Rio Olympics rose to 28%, as compared with 20% in 2012. This is four times the percentage of the population attending private schools. From one private school alone, Millfield in Somerset, six ex-pupils represented the UK at the Rio Olympics.[49] This seamless social reproduction is facilitated by family wealth, but also by the much better resource levels in the private as compared to the state school sector, as Table 2.1 shows.

Table 2.1: Educational outcomes: state versus private sector

	UK	UK (maintained schools)	UK (Independent schools)
Average PISA score	500	497	516
Socio-economic background	0.20	0.16	0.46
Native	0.93	0.94	0.91
Speak national language at home	0.98	0.98	0.97
Students per teacher	14.5	14.9	9.5
Quality of resources (index)	0.45	0.44	0.61
Residency not considered in admittance	0.19	0.17	0.35
Academic performance not considered in admittance	0.72	0.84	0.00

Source: OECD, 2011, PISA database.

In the table we can see that while pupil–teacher ratios in the state sector are 15 to 1, in the private sector they are less than

10 to 1, while at the same time the quality of resources in the private sector is far higher than that in state schools.

The new diversified and divisive state sector

However, private schools are the tip of an iceberg of educational privilege. Even within the state sector there are significant class inequalities. The Organisation for Economic Co-operation and Development (OECD) found that middle-class students tend to be taught in smaller classes and have access to better-quality teaching resources than do their working-class peers.[50] They are also more likely than their working-class peers to attend the grant maintained sector within state schooling. The grant maintained sector covers a range of schools that enjoy some form of separation from the mainstream state sector while continuing to derive large parts (if not all) of their income from the public purse. From church schools to city academies to the free schools, schools in the grant maintained sector effectively impose restrictions on entry, selecting pupils with characteristics that they regard as desirable.

Box 2.1: Academies and free schools

Academies differ substantially from local authority-run comprehensives. They are funded directly through central government, operate outside local authority control and determine their own employment conditions. The New Labour government of 1997–2010 introduced academies, targeting mainly at deprived urban areas. The Coalition government of 2010–15 rapidly accelerated New Labour's programme. In 2010 when New Labour left office there were 203 academies; as of June 2016 there were 5,302 academies, and by September 2016 there were 429 free schools.[51] Free schools are a further attempt to entrench a supply of schools outside of local authority control.[52] They operate with pedagogic and financial freedoms, with separate admissions procedures, and, as Ferrari and Green argue, are intended to stimulate more competition in education provision.[53]

The existence of both a private sector and a selective grant-maintained sector funded by the state completely undermines comprehensivisation and is hard to reconcile with the principles of social justice. But the British public have a long history of tolerating a system that was set up to better their betters, and is still extremely successful at doing just that. In his Fabian Society booklet *Politicians, Equality, and Comprehensives*, Dennis Marsden argued that it was difficult to sell the idea of 'the common school for all' to an electorate that had shown itself to be largely indifferent to the social divisiveness of the educational system.[54] A poll in 1957 had shown that only 10% of the UK public felt that segregated education was socially undesirable.[55] So, despite the torrent of educational policy changes in the 20 years since 1997, it appears that some things remain the same as they were 70 years ago. One consequence of the continuing high tolerance of elitism and unfairness in the educational system is that, under contemporary neoliberalism, divisive and unfair perspectives have become enshrined in educational policy rather than being challenged and changed. As Nick Stevenson argues, we are currently seeing the breaking up of the comprehensive system and its rapid replacement by an academy system that is both more selective and more fragmented than the system it replaces, as well as less democratic.[56] James Meek points out that both Labour and Conservative governments have been involved in a process of semi-privatisation of education that leaves it 'ripe for the introduction of flat fees for usage in the future'. Meek suggests that one word to describe it might be 'autonomisation' – the process by which state-run bodies continue to be funded by the state but are run autonomously on a non-profit basis.[57] However, Johnson and Mansell in their TUC research report are more blunt. They assert that 'England's school system may already be well on the way to having been privatised, over a comparatively short period of time and with very little public debate'.[58]

The autonomy of academies is a strange creature. It results in less rather than more autonomy for the teachers who work in academies. As Johnson and Mansell point out, they are frequently expected to teach to a prescribed model, and in some cases exactly to the model provided by the academy chain provider.[59] Academies also often claim autonomy in relation to equalities issues, which in effect becomes a failure to stick to equalities principles. This can leave their staff feeling that they have nowhere to go to deal with problems in relation to work conditions. As Johnson and Mansell conclude, this kind of autonomy is a system weakness rather than a strength. It also results in some dubious funding decisions. As Sir Michael Wilshaw, head of Ofsted at the time, told the House of Commons Education Committee when giving evidence on multi-academy trusts in June 2016, in the seven failing multi-academy trusts that Ofsted had inspected at that point, £110 million was being spent on consultancies, an average of £10 million per trust each year. Wilshaw reasonably raised the issue of why those failing multi-academy trusts were not spending this money on pupils rather than consultants.

As he asserted:

> When we looked at the seven failing academy trusts, they had a philosophy that was what I describe as a Walmart philosophy or, 'Pile them high, sell them cheap. Let's empire build rather than have the capacity to improve these schools.'[60]

This sounds like a philosophy of commercialisation and marketing rather than anything to do with education, and one that is clearly not doing anything to improve educational provision. Wilshaw concluded:

> We were doing a survey on good, well performing, multi-academy trusts – and we were struggling to find them, quite honestly. We have established half a dozen good ones, but there are some very mediocre trusts.[61]

As is evident from Table 2.2, despite the mission of the academies programme to drive up educational standards, between 2012 and March 2016, 81% of local authority schools were found to be Good or Outstanding, as compared to 73% of academies.

What the evidence points to is that if every school in the country became an academy the result would be little or no difference in the standards of the educational system or in the class gap in educational achievement. While academisation is

Table 2.2: Analysis of Ofsted inspection by school type

	LA maintained schools	Academies	Sponsored academies	Converter academies	Free schools
Outstanding	1,232	394	63	331	39
Good	8,474	1,376	410	966	74
Requires improvement	2,089	554	302	252	26
Inadequate	171	115	64	51	4
Total	11,966	2,439	839	1,600	143
% Good and outstanding	*81%*	*73%*	*56%*	*81%*	*79%*

Source: House of Commons Education Committee, 2016, Analysis of Ofsted Inspections by school type, from written evidence by the Local Government Association.

branded in terms of raising educational achievement, the real agenda is privatisation.

As well as failing to drive up standards, academies are also more selective than state comprehensive schools. Academy schools were found to be flouting admission rules by selecting pupils from more privileged families, according to a major study of the programme. In its report the Academies Commission said that it had received 'numerous submissions' stating that academies were finding methods to 'select covertly' and warned that this could lead to increased social segregation.[62] Its fears are supported by a Europe-wide survey that reported that more school autonomy in relation to admissions resulted in higher levels of social segregation between schools.[63] Although research on the earlier academies[64] found little evidence either way in relation to segregation, research from the National Pupil Database revealed that 51% of more recently established academies took less than half of their fair share of FSM students.[65] Research by Gorard in 2016 found a direct relationship between increased diversity of schooling and the increased social class segregation of FSM children, and concluded that social class segregation 'is associated with greater unfairness in practice, worse opportunities for the most disadvantaged, lowered aspirations, and lower participation in later education'.[66]

Free schools: an ideological rather than an educational initiative

The original rationale for free schools was devolution of power to the local community. They were supposed to be locally developed by parents, teachers and community groups, but are now more likely to be handed over to academy chains. At the time when they were introduced in 2010 the Department for Education described them as 'all-ability state-funded schools set up in response to what local people say they want and need in order to improve education for children in their community'.[67] But free schools are not only far less democratic than the hype surrounding them claims, they are also more selective than ordinary state schools. While nationally 16.7% of children are entitled to claim FSM because their household income is below £16,000, in free schools the percentage of claimants is 10%. In the most extreme example, one primary free school had just 3.4% of pupils eligible for FSM, as compared with 43.7% of primary age children across the local authority where it was located.[68] As the National Audit Office concluded,[69] free schools have a negative effect on surrounding schools, creaming off more privileged students, and provide poor value for money.

So, we are seeing radical changes in the state educational system in England; changes that are transforming the purposes of education, the ways in which it is funded, teaching and learning and, inevitably, relationships between teachers and taught.

I want now to look briefly at some statistics that make clear the polarisation within the current system, before examining the growing unfair distribution of resources within the state sector. The 2013 Organisation for Economic Co-operation and Development (OECD) report concluded that schools in England are among the most socially segregated in the developed world. The report found that England had unusually high levels of segregation in terms of poor and migrant families being concentrated in the same schools. Particularly worrying were the statistics on working-class minority ethnic families. Eighty per cent were taught in schools with high concentrations of other immigrant or disadvantaged students – the highest proportion in the developed world.[70] As a more recent report found, 61% of ethnic minority children in England – and 90% in London –

begin Year 1 in schools where ethnic minorities are the majority of the pupil body.[71]

As Table 2.3 shows, 21% of all primary schools in London exhibit significant levels of class and ethnic segregation. The figure rises to an average of 44% for all 'faith schools'. But this is more than a London-based problem. Half of FSM pupils are found in just a fifth of all schools.[72]

Table 2.3: Significantly segregated primary schools, London

| Type | Denomination | Segregated schools | | All schools | | | |
		n	%	n	%	Index	Penetration
Foundation		5	1	43	2	55	0.12
Community		157	41	1,284	70	58	0.12
Voluntary controlled	Church of England	3	1	17	1	84	0.18
Voluntary aided	Church of England	67	17	221	12	145	0.30
Voluntary aided	Roman Catholic	134	35	242	13	264	0.55
Voluntary aided	Other	18	5	23	1	373	0.78

Source: Poverty Site, 2015.

Funding and the failure to achieve fairness

In the two years from April 2010 to March 2012 the government spent £8.3 billion on the academies project. This was £1 billion over budget. Some of this money came from the £95 million originally intended for improving underperforming schools.[73] Although the House of Commons Committee of Public Accounts did not spell out the implications in terms of fairness and social justice, this was a redistribution from the predominantly working-class students in underperforming comprehensives to the more privileged cohort of students attending academies. As Austin Mitchell, MP, succinctly argued:

you are taking money – first of all £95 million originally allocated to school improvement. That is hitting the poorer schools isn't it? Those are the schools that really need improving. You are taking a similar amount – that's £400 million – from funds for intervention in underperforming schools. In other words you are hitting the poor to help the better off.[74]

Figure 2.1: Funding per pupil at state-maintained and academy primary schools

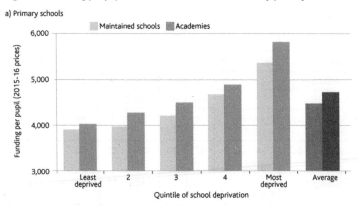

a) Primary schools

Source: Sibieta, 2015.

Figure 2.2: Funding per pupil at state-maintained and academy secondary schools

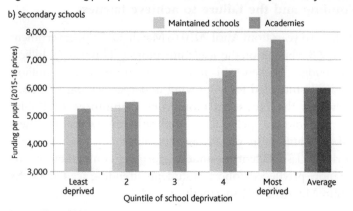

b) Secondary schools

Source: Sibieta, 2015.

Figures 2.1 and 2.2 provide more details on overall levels of unfair funding in relation to academies and state comprehensives. However, within the academy sector, considerably more secondary schools have low levels of FSM students than have medium and high levels: 1,818, as compared to 149 with medium levels and only 58 with high levels of FSM pupils. At the primary stage the numbers are 352 schools with low levels of FSM pupils, as compared to 67 with medium levels and just 29 with high levels of FSM students.[75] At secondary level in London this translates to 58% of academies with low levels of FSM pupils, as compared to 42.9% of state comprehensives.[76] So, the redistribution from state schools to academies is, in effect, as Austin Mitchell pointed out, a redistribution from the poor to the relatively well-off.

But this unfair redistribution was not just in relation to academies. As one of the Public Accounts Committee members pointed out, at least £2.3 million had been spent on free schools that either had failed to open or had very few pupils.[77] This was happening at a time when the then Coalition government had cut the education budget by more than £5 billion.

This unfair situation in relation to free schools has continued. England's free schools received 60% more funding per pupil than local authority primaries and secondaries in 2013/14. In the latest figures available from the Department for Education (2015), the average amount of state funding given to free schools was £7,761, as compared with a national figure for local authority schools of £4,767.[78] By 2015 free school funding was double the original estimates, at a time when many school buildings in the state maintained sector were in poor condition.[79] So, free schools, like the academies, are receiving a disproportionate share of education funding, despite having lower levels of working-class children than state maintained schools. The latest statistics also show that places at free schools are considerably more expensive to provide than local authority school places.[80] A place in a primary free school opening in 2013/14 or 2014/15 cost on average £14,400, or 33% more than a place created in the same years in a local authority primary school, while a place in a secondary free school cost £19,000 (or 51% more).

A pattern of the schools with more privileged pupils (in terms of FSM intake) having better funding levels also operates within the state school sector, and is set to continue. Table 2.4 highlights some clear differences according to deprivation. In 2015/16 local authorities with low levels of FSM pupils received a slightly higher average funding increase (2.9%) than those with high levels of FSM (0.3%).

Table 2.4: Changes in local authority funding per pupil by level of deprivation, 2015/16

Local authority type	Average increase (%)	Proportion of local authorities with an increase in funding (%)
Least deprived	2.9	84
2nd quintile	1.9	68
Middle quintile	0.9	38
4th quintile	0.6	23
Most deprived	0.3	13
All local authorities	1.3	54

Source: Sibieta, 2015.

Schools are now experiencing real-terms cuts in spending per pupil. Proposals in 2017 imply a real-terms cut in school spending per pupil of about 7% between 2014/15 and 2019/20. This rises to 9% if we account for increases in staff National Insurance and pension contributions and to 12% if we also account for the Office for Budget Responsibility's assumptions on likely growth in public sector earnings. The funding proposals of all three main political parties are much less generous than the small real-terms increases in spending per pupil that were experienced over earlier Parliaments. However, what appears to have remained the same is the preferential funding treatment of academies and free schools. A further continuity is that it is primarily working-class schools that will suffer the worst underfunding. As Morton argues, schools with the most deprived children will be worst hit in the government's proposed reallocation of the existing overall schools' budget. She draws on statistics to show that primary schools with high number of working-class pupils would lose an estimated £578 per pupil.[81] Reinforcing Morton's findings, current research by the NUT and Child Poverty Action Group using Department for Education (DfE) data shows that, under current government school funding policy, the 1,000 schools with the highest number of children with FSM are facing much deeper cuts in funding per pupil than schools generally.[82] Their research shows that primary schools with over 40% of children on FSM will on average lose £473 per pupil in real terms, or £140 more than the average for primary schools generally. In secondary schools with over 40% of children on FSM, the average loss per pupil will be £803, or a staggering £326 more than the average for secondary schools as a whole. So, already disadvantaged working-class students will be further disadvantaged in relation to their middle-class peers. Yet, research shows that additional expenditure has large effects on educational attainment. Gibbons et al found that improvements in school funding in urban primary schools made a real difference to pupil achievement, despite policy makers and media commentators often suggesting that it does not. They also found that the effects of expenditure tended to be higher in working-class schools.[83]

Conclusion

The divide in English education is no longer just between state and private but, increasingly, within the state sector itself. In the next chapter I investigate what these growing divisions mean for working-class experiences of education in the 21st century. I explore how a diversity of types of schooling has affected working-class experiences in education by drawing on evidence from both my own and other academics' research. Although all children suffer from a hyper-competitive, excessively hierarchical educational system, the symbolic violence enacted in and through the educational system does not impact on all children equally. In relation to the degree of educational and emotional damage inflicted, there is something else that also remains the same: it is predominantly working-class children who suffer the most. The educational system is eroding all children's freedom to learn, but it is still working-class children who have the least opportunities for fulfilling learning that can realise their potential. Whereas in the past the damage came through failing the 11-plus and being relegated to schools that were seen to be second rate, now working-class children, although nominally receiving the same education as their middle-class peers who go to state schools, are subject to a narrowing of the curriculum[84] and a degree of teaching to the test that is not experienced by their middle-class peers. They are also attending schools that are relatively less well funded than the schools attended by middle-class children. I examine the impact of these conditions on working-class children's learning in the next two chapters.

THREE

Working-class educational experiences

In this chapter I focus internally on the workings of the educational system, and what these have meant for working-class educational experiences. The key points of the chapter are illustrated through a number of case studies, mainly from young people whom I interviewed between 2000 and 2016 for a range of different research projects, but also from a working-class parent, Josie, whom I interviewed six times over a period of 20 years. But before I look at the lived experiences of working-class students and their parents I want to present an up-to-date snapshot of the social class attainment gap. Over the three years 2011/12 to 2013/14 disadvantaged students (those on FSM, in receipt of pupil premium and nearly all working class) were 27% less likely to achieve five or more GCSE grades A*–C including English and Maths (Table 3.1).

Table 3.1: Key Stage 4 attainment gap for 2012–14

Percentage of pupils achieving 5 or more grades A*-C including GCSE English and Mathematics

	2011/12	2012/13	2013/14
Disadvantaged pupils	38.5	40.9	36.5
All other pupils	65.7	67.9	64.0
All pupils	58.8	60.6	56.6
Percentage point gap	27.2	26.9	27.4

Note: 2013/14 figures were added to this table in a refresh of this documant on 29 January 2015.
Source: DfE statistical working paper 'Measuring disadvantaged pupils' attainment gaps over time', 19 December 2014 (updated 29 January 2015).

The most recent statistics from the DfE (April 2017) present a bleak contrast between the poorest children on FSM and those from families with incomes of £78,000 and above: an attainment gap of 47% (Figure 3.1).

Figure 3.1: Achievement of 5+ A*–C grade GCSEs including English and Maths, by income

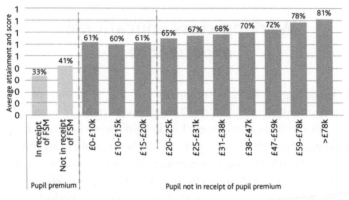

Source: DfE, 2017.

Figure 3.2: Percentage of high-achieving children by family background for selected countries

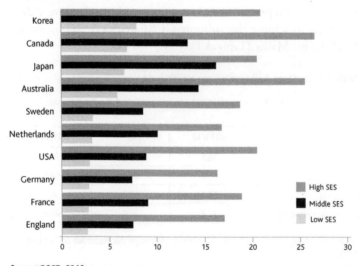

Source: OECD, 2010.

If we then consider how this compares with other nations across the globe we find that in 2009 England was bottom of the league table for the percentage of working-class children achieving high academic levels (Figure 3.2).

This is the scale of the problem confronted by those concerned with the class gap in educational attainment; and it is this gap that the new diversity in educational provision – academies, free schools and now super grammar schools – is intended to address.

Academies: working miracles in deprived areas?

The hype surrounding academies is that they will address the social class attainment gap displayed in Table 3.1. They have been heavily promoted as a means of pulling up working-class achievement. In 2008, six years after the first academies were opened, Andrew Adonis claimed that academies were 'establishing a culture of ambition to replace the poverty of aspiration'.[1] In 2012 the then Prime Minister, David Cameron, claimed that they were 'working miracles in some of the most deprived parts of our country'.[2] So, the political rhetoric is all about improving both working-class achievement and working-class experiences of education. Yet the reality is much murkier. As Bailey and Ball point out, 18 academy chains have now been prevented from opening new schools because their performance and management abilities have been substandard, and 68 academies have received warning letters from the DfE about their poor performance.[3] So the political hype surrounding academies' transforming of working-class underachievement has turned out to be just that – political hype.

In interviews I conducted between 2010 and 2016 working-class students refer much more to what gets in the way of their learning in academies rather than to what enhances it. Tania talked about her excitement when a Performing Arts Academy opened half a mile from her home. She had done a BTEC qualification in Performing Arts and said, "at first I was so excited. I thought it was so tempting, the idea of a school that mainly focuses on the things I am most interested in. It felt amazing to be going there." Tania did go, but only for three days. She said, "I actually hated it, it was like a military camp, you had to walk in silence, chant these mantras, wear suits. The last straw was when one of my best friends was asked to leave after the second day for talking in the corridor." Tania expressed incredulity about the way teaching and learning were organised in the school. She told me, "I did try and talk to my head of year. I said, 'how can kids express themselves when there are all these rules?', and he said, 'but this is what they do in Detroit, this is what they do in Harlem, and they get results'. And I was, like, this is unbelievable what sort of results can you get when none of the kids are allowed to express themselves?"

What this reminded me of was schools for the working classes set up at the beginning of state education for all, whose primary mission was to control and pacify rather than to educate and stimulate. It also resonates with Christie Kulz's findings in her ethnography of an academy in North London. She quotes the head teacher's rationale for what some of the schools' parents called its 'draconian' rules:

> What underpins this philosophy, is that if they come
> from unstructured backgrounds where anything goes
> and rules and boundaries are not clear in their home,
> we need to ensure that they're clear here. So we run
> very tight systems here, you could call it a traditional
> approach or a formal approach.[4]

Underlying his words is a sense of the working-class home as one that is out of control, 'where anything goes'. You are also left with the feeling that at times this is as much about punishment as it is about education. As one of the students told Kulz, "we used to call here the prison because it actually did seem like that sometimes". This is the Boot Camp model of schooling for the working classes, military camps for the undisciplined masses. Jessica Abrahams writes about the sense of shock she felt as a researcher in an academy as she began to feel 'the full force of what it must feel like to be a working-class child in an authoritarian Academy school, where rules are rigid and exceptions are not made, where your culture is disregarded and your home circumstances ignored, where you cannot challenge authority and are often made to feel small, insignificant and powerless'.[5]

Comprehensive only in name

But these are the schools that are often seen as 'good', providing the educational backbone that the working classes are seen to lack. There are other schools, either in areas where there are still grammar schools or else urban comprehensives in deprived localities, forced to compete in hyper-competitive educational markets that are seen to be beyond redemption not just by the middle and upper classes but often by the working-class children who attend them. These are frequently the schools languishing at the bottom of local authority league tables, and often the social class segregation they suffer is compounded by racial segregation. There is a long and notorious history of labelling ethnically diverse comprehensive schools with a predominance of working-class students as 'bog-standard'[6] or 'sink'[7] comprehensives. Stereotyping and labelling were also evident in the vast majority of the interviews carried out with middle-class parents and children. So, for example:

Chiltern is like a rubbish dump school, all the girls who go there are slags. (Emma, White English, middle-class girl)

All the kids that go to Sutton Boys smell, they're all tramps. (Marcus, White English, middle-class boy)

Working-class bodies are marked as degenerate or deficient or, in many cases, both. There were also shades of paranoia; a fear of contamination in which mixing with the 'rough' children is seen to pollute 'nice' sons and daughters who risk being led astray or worse:

My mum said if I go to Chiltern I'll turn bad cos all the kids there are bad. (Marcus, White English, middle-class boy)

If Hamlyn doesn't take me my dad's going to appeal and if they still don't take me I have to move to Oxford because he said all

the schools here are rubbish and the kids are all thick. (Arabella,
White English, middle-class girl)

Such attitudes, and the fear of 'the class other' that underpins
them, have resulted in a growing number of urban comprehensives
becoming pathologised working-class schools, and I discuss the
emotional impact this has on how the working-class children
who attend them see themselves, both as learners and in relation
to others, in Chapter Seven. An added concern is that these
schools are not only seen as unacceptable school choices for
the upper and middle classes but also, increasingly, have an
impoverished curriculum. The Royal Society's Open Public
Services Network report found that 'the curriculum taught to
children in poorer parts of Britain is significantly different to
that taught in wealthier areas', resulting in restricted educational
opportunities for working-class children.[8]

The general view is that secondary moderns are a thing of
the past. But the demonised places of working-class educational
failure that they represented are still with us. They are to be found
both in the 'sink' working-class comprehensives that I have been
writing about and in the bottom sets and streams that I discuss
in the next chapter. The very different social composition of
comprehensive schools, and the growth of setting and streaming
within them, has resulted in a majority of comprehensives being
comprehensive only in name.

The standards agenda that is making the lives of so many
students and teachers a misery has nothing to do with the
educational needs of students. It is primarily a political project
for education in relation to national competitiveness and the
demands of globalisation.[9] The colossal increase of setting and
streaming has had further negative repercussions for working-class
education. If we are to see the real power of schooling on class
identity and identification we need to consider the development
since the mid-1980s of increasing systems of assessment and
setting and streaming in schools. The all-consuming focus on
testing and measuring has served to re-emphasise and valorise
ability as measured on test scores as the 'be-all and end-all' of
education.[10]

As a white, middle-class mother whom I interviewed commented:

> *I mean, in our school there are generally speaking six to eight sets for each subject. She was either in sets 1 or 2 for most of them. What kids in set 8 were doing, I don't know. I mean they probably didn't even sit GCSEs, even kids in sets 5 and 6 probably didn't get Cs. Those people at the bottom would have fulfilled only the expectations of the teachers for that set. The problem with setting to that extent, which we didn't appreciate, is that they only fulfil the expectations of the set at the end of the day, they don't seem to move.* (Joanna, white, middle-class mother)

It also makes a mockery of the so-called comprehensive system that it is still claimed that we have in England. As another white, middle-class mother explained, her initial concerns about poor behaviour and ill discipline had been ill founded because her daughter's comprehensive "is very keen to separate out the sheep from the goats, you know to make sure nothing gets in the way of the bright children's learning".

A curriculum that marginalises working-class knowledge?

In English society, any critical engagement or creativity in formal schooling, especially for those in the years of GCSE preparation, has increasingly become the preserve of the upper and middle classes. In a research project I conducted in 2012 on the educational experiences of working-class young people in a period of austerity,[11] it was evident that learning out of school was seen as both more rewarding and relevant than school-based learning. However, it is important to point out from the outset that these activities were very different in both variety and purpose from the often expensive activities underpinned by an objective of concerted cultivation that the middle and upper classes were regularly engaged in. (These will be discussed in Chapter Six.) A small number of working-class young people, who often had damaged learner identities in school, had succeeded in creating supportive social networks through engaging in a range of out-of-school activities, mostly connected to sports. In the process they had frequently acquired social and cultural capital, as well as useful practical knowledge. It was this minority of working-class young people who described taking part in a variety of out-of-school activities who conveyed a sense of passion, motivation and the critical engagement that was missing from their descriptions of school learning. So Ricky talks about 'his adventurous side', which is expressed not through school but in the many things he does outside of school: cricket, cycling, rugby, skating, fishing and making things with his hands. Asked to describe his most exciting learning experiences, he told me:

> When I was about 9 or 10 I made a bicycle out of wood by myself and then when I was 10 I built a cupboard for me mum. Well, me and my dad made a cupboard out of wood and stuff like that for over our stairs so we could put our towels and stuff in it. And that's when I was 10 and it is still up there now.

In the following extract Shianne describes her latest outing with the Air Cadets. It is clear that among the excitement and fun involved there is also a great deal of learning taking place, academic as well as practical.

> I am in this thing called Air Cadets, so I went with them and er ... We have to get all kitted up with helmets and gloves and parachute and stuff like that. And I was flying it, and you get to do, like, acrobats and tricks and flips and stuff like that. And I got to control the plane and then I got to do a flip with it. And then we did this thing where ...You know in space they have no gravity ... We did that in the cockpit of our plane, so there is no gravity, then I took my glove off and let it float about, and then everything was floating about. And then we went back to gravity and everything just come back down again. So it was fun and then I had to land the plane as well.

When asked about school-based science, however, Shianne claimed "I hate it, it's boring". Rather, such young people, with damaged and tenuous learner identities in school, managed to nurture interests, talents, and valued identities in their activities outside school.

A possible clue to this disjuncture between enjoyment and engagement in out-of-school activities and an instrumentalised accommodation to school-based learning lies in the very different language young people used to describe such experiences. Out-of-school activities are characterised by collaboration and collectivity. School, in contrast, was seen to be more about failure than success, a race to beat your friends that often felt to these young people like a 'no-win situation'. As Pritti pointed out, "you feel bad if you do a lot better than your friends cos you've shown them up and they think you are a geek, and you feel bad if you do badly cos you've let yourself down". Part of the systemic problem here, which became increasingly obvious as I spoke to more working-class students, was that the subjects and activities they enjoyed, and often excelled at, had little status and recognition within the current educational system. This suggests, as Jessica Gerrard has argued, that working-class educational activities occur through diverse forms that are not immediately identified by, let alone incorporated into, the formal educational system.[12] Furthermore, this failure within education to respect and value working-class knowledge has resulted in the invidious divide between vocational and academic knowledge.

Vocational education has a long history of stigmatisation – stereotyped and devalued as education desired by, and more suitable for, children of the working classes. As a result, in Britain it has always approximated to what John Dewey called 'narrow technical trade education for specialized callings, carried on under the control of others',[13] a restricted, a-theoretical type of apprenticeship. Unsurprisingly, attempts to upgrade vocational education have failed because the British middle classes have never countenanced it as appropriate education for their own children.[14] Despite a great deal of rhetoric about high-status vocational routes, policies have always been directed at the lower- and, indeed, lowest-achieving young people.[15] Any sort of equality between vocational and academic education would require a transformation in both what vocational education constitutes and who engages in it.

It is unsurprising, then, that vocational education in England is working-class education. A study that examined the degree of democratic participation among young people who had been educated in vocational streams in England, Denmark and Germany[16] found that inequalities in democratic engagement are increased by allocating young people to different tracks on the basis of what is described as their ability. This was particularly noticeable in England, the country where vocational tracks had the lowest status. The English vocational students described the powerlessness they felt when it came to influencing wider political and social issues:

> There's nothing we can say about it because to them we're no one, we're a nobody. (Julie)

> I think that no matter what my point of view is, it's not going to change anything. (Sam)

> We're not looked at, us little people, we're not; I just wish something could be done about bad things, but nothing ever can because that's life. (Jane)[17]

What is also striking is the sense of abjection, and the feelings of worthlessness they display. The authors conclude that 'prior experiences of inequalities in the educational system, such as prior placement in vocational tracks, which also included unfair treatment and selective processes appear to be associated with lower levels of confidence, self-value, and aspiration'.

The growing out-sourcing of educational work to the home and its consequences

Both the continued failure to develop vocational education that has equivalent value with academic education, and the frenzied preoccupation with introducing greater and greater diversity within school supply, have degraded and diminished working-class education. But equally significant in terms of impact on working-class experiences of education since the mid-1980s has been the growing out-sourcing of educational learning to the home. This has happened at a historical period when working-class parents have become increasingly responsible for reversing educational inequality and overcoming structural constraints. In the 21st century responsibility for educational success has been recast as more of a family matter and less of a collective or social responsibility.[18] As a consequence, parents, and particularly mothers, are now expected to become home-based teachers of their children. Of course many do not have the time, and here we see an enormous growth in out-of-school activities and private tuition for children. But many, and especially working-class parents, have neither the money to pay for others to teach their children nor the expertise or confidence to do it themselves. In the following case study, Josie, a white, working-class woman whom I interviewed six times over 20 years, explains why, despite all her efforts and aspirations for her two sons, they both express the same sense of failure about their schooling that she experienced in relation to her own.

Josie is someone I have remained in contact with over a period of 25 years. I first interviewed her in 1994. She is a lone mother whose Italian parents migrated to the UK to work in the garment industry. Both Josie's parents had left school before they were 14, while she left her London comprehensive at age 16 with "just a handful of certificates". In the first interview she described a poignant example of misunderstanding and incomprehension from what she called "the worst day of many awful days I spent in primary school".

There was one day in primary school where I'd been asking about a subject and the teacher was telling me and I kept on asking because I still couldn't understand and on the third occasion she made me leave the classroom and I had to stand outside the door. I stood there and after half an hour a girl came out and said "The teacher says you can come in if you apologise". Then she shut the door. I stood there thinking what does apologise mean. I didn't know what the teacher wanted me to do so I just didn't know what to do. If she had said, you know, "sorry", but I didn't know what apologise meant. The teacher came out after half an hour later and said "You can come if you apologise", then shut the door, didn't give me time to ask her. She left me there all day.

In the end she came out. She was furious with me and she shook me. "How dare you not apologise." I just burst into tears. I felt so awful. She went "Uhm". I said "I don't know what apologise means", so she said, "Oh, it means sorry". I said, "Well, I'm sorry." As if, you know, if I'd have known what it meant … I was just too embarrassed to go in. I was only seven and it was a class of 35 children and she'd be standing there saying "Come on, apologise" and me not knowing what apologise meant. I daren't go in. So it was a whole lot of misunderstanding.

Here Josie's sense of being out of place and misunderstood is potent, the implicit values and standards of the educational system appear incomprehensible and her feelings of not belonging are starkly reinforced by being made to stand outside the classroom for the whole day. It is perhaps unsurprising that later in the interview she told me:

My whole sense of myself when I was at school was that I was no good at anything, that I was hopeless at learning.

Josie's narrative stresses over and over again the importance of education, her personal feelings of incompetence and how her lack of confidence worked against her undertaking any educational activity with a sense of efficacy in relation to her two sons. For Josie, parental involvement neither came naturally nor could be taken for granted. It had to be worked for extremely hard. This hard work was particularly evident in relation to Darren, who was falling behind the rest of the children in his Year 5 class in reading and writing:

I have tried, I really have. I knew I should be playing a role in getting Darren to read but I wasn't qualified. Therefore it put extra pressure on me because I was no good at reading myself, it was too important for me to handle and I'd get very upset and angry at Darren.

Josie's high levels of anxiety that Darren would repeat her experience of educational failure were palpable. She scheduled a regular reading session with Darren every evening, which she said she had "come to dread". She knew she had to give Darren enough time to attempt the words he didn't know but, as she went on to admit, "it winds me up so much". It also reminded her of her own tortuous attempts to master reading and writing when she was at primary school. As she ruefully reflected:

> *What was happening was I thought if my son can't read he's going to go through exactly the same thing as me, and yet he's had a better start because he knows the language, and that's what's really upsetting me cos if I was coming across heavy it was because of my anxieties. I thought, oh no, he's not going through what I went through.*

A tangible sense of desperation is apparent in her account of trying to do Darren's homework herself when she discovers that "he hadn't done it properly". She laughed wryly as she described how she had got into such a state because of his English homework that she had got up in the middle of the night, gone through his school bag, and once she had found his English homework, sat there with Tippex and a dictionary, "because my own spelling is hopeless", erasing the spelling mistakes and replacing them with the correct spelling. As she went on to explain:

> *I find it really difficult helping Darren with his work. I'm the wrong person for it because I am already angry in myself because of my own education and how that sort of progressed, and all the problems I had to go through, all the embarrassment and humiliation.*

As Josie pointed out, her relationship with her two boys was generally good, and she wanted her time with them to be positive and rewarding, but anxieties, fears and pressures around school achievement felt like "a black cloud over our heads". As she vividly describes in the following quote, at times she "just explode[s] with the anxiety of it all".

> *I have ended up screaming and shouting and we've had bad rows about it. I'd have put him off altogether so I've had to back off*

and let the school take it on. I'm the wrong person to teach him because of the emotional state I get into.

Attempting to get the school to listen to her concerns also had unpredictable and upsetting consequences:

I always found if I went to the class teacher, she'd take it very personal and think I was attacking her. I wasn't. I was just bringing it to her attention in case she didn't know, you know, that in my opinion he's not progressing. The way I see him and from what I expect of him I don't see the progress. But I'd say "I'm not saying that it's because you're not teaching my son. I do realise you have a class of 30 and you're only one person and you do so much and you're expected to do a lot of other things because the National Curriculum expects so much of you. I do understand about that. But what can I do about his reading?" But when I did go to the class teachers I think they took it too personal and felt I was attacking them when really it was that it is so important I couldn't let it go.

As Josie commented, "every time I go into school I come away thinking they are speaking a different language", which must have plunged her straight back into her own school experiences.

Throughout my interviews with Josie she talked of being "fobbed off" and feeling that she was "talking to a brick wall". Yet, because of her own sense of educational inadequacy the school had come to be perceived as "the last and only resort". Her personal history of immigration, working-class background and academic failure resulted in a sense that there were no other options.

When I went to see his teacher I was pretty upset about Darren not reading and it may have come across like "how come Darren's not reading. If you aren't hearing him read what are you doing then?" I was maybe coming across like that but what I meant was can he possibly have some extra time. Can someone here, for God's sake, give him some extra reading and let him get on because it's making my life harder. I was getting so anxious about him not reading cos I couldn't really help him. I'd get upset and frustrated and it wasn't doing Darren any good because if he can't read what was happening?

In the last interview Josie reminded me that when she actually got to see the head teacher she had promised her that Darren would leave primary school being able to read fluently, and that if he couldn't Josie had every right to come back and complain. But, as Josie pointed out, ist was too late by then, and by the time he left primary school Darren was firmly on track for the educational failure she had experienced in her own schooling. There is no need for me to spell out the powerful sense of unfairness lurking beneath Josie's words, because she goes on to provide her own cogent summary of how increasing reliance on parental involvement within the British educational system is perpetuating educational inequalities:

> *You need parental involvement. You need parents to be able to complement what you're doing but that's all it should be. It shouldn't be any more. You see not all people speak English, not all parents read and write, so how can they help their children at home. They're at a disadvantage anyway so when they come to school they've got to have the help there. You should just be able to say to the teacher "Look, I can't do it. You're qualified, can you do something about it?" without the teacher getting all upset about it. There's a lot of parents who can't, just can't do it.*

Here Josie powerfully resists a construction of herself as her children's teacher. This resistance about assuming a teaching role was both justified and understandable. It was related to a variety of factors: her own extremely negative experiences of schooling, the resulting feelings that she lacked educational competencies, the refusal of her children to see her as an educational expert and the amount of time she had available to undertake educational work in the home. When her two boys were at primary school she had two insecure clerical jobs that left her with little time for schoolwork. By the time her sons were both at secondary school Josie had lost both jobs and was surviving on a number of casualised, low-paid cleaning jobs.

Josie was caught in a double bind. She felt inadequate to support her sons educationally, but she was also unsuccessful in her efforts to get the school staff to provide Darren with extra support. In her interview with me, Darren's Year 5 teacher described Josie as "far too needy, aggressive, and over-emotional". In the much more middle-class school I was also researching in at the time, mothers were regularly labelled as over-emotional, although assertive rather than aggressive. They, however, nearly always got their demands met for extra educational provision and support. The mother of the one boy who was struggling with reading managed to gain daily one-to-one reading support for him and told me that she wouldn't expect anything less. He was also receiving two paid sessions of private English tuition a week.

The contrast with Josie's situation was glaring. When I asked what social activities the boys were involved in out of school Josie laughed. "You've got to be joking, social activities cost money, that's why I haven't got a social life. I can't afford to go out." Josie's case study encapsulates the class inequalities in parental involvement. Material resources, educational knowledge, parents' own educational experiences and the amount of domestic and educational support parents, and in particular mothers, had access to, add up to an important class difference that impacted on their relationship to their children's education and the texture of their involvement in schooling. And it is important to point out, just as one of Jackson and Marsden's interviewees did in the 1960s, that it is mainly mothers who undertake the work of educating children. But the major difference between now and when Jackson and Marsden were writing in the 1960s is that state schooling increasingly relies on learning outside of school, at a time when resources to enable this are very unequally distributed across the social classes.

The last time I interviewed Josie, in 2016, both boys were grown up and in their early 30s. Darren still had a clerical job in the Benefits Office he had joined when leaving school at 16, and had his own one-bedroomed local authority flat, just over two miles away from where his mother lived. Dean was unemployed, living with his mother and on disability benefit. She said mournfully:

> *I had high hopes of Dean, he was such a good boy, worked so hard at school, not like Darren who was always losing it. He got 4s in his SATs, I thought he's not going to turn out like me and his dad, but then he went more and more into himself at secondary school, then he stopped eating and got really ill when he was in Year 10, and to be honest he has never really recovered, it's been all ups and downs since then.*

Josie spent a long time explaining about the many hours she spent trying to get appropriate support for Dean through both educational and social services. She said "it was a bit like Darren all over again because I knew I wasn't the right person to help him. I was running round in circles trying to get the right help when I just didn't have the knowledge. It turned out he had Body Dysmorphic Disorder". She laughed ironically – "another word I had never heard of". Throughout Josie's story we gain a powerful sense of how difficult it is to put your child over hurdles you have failed to clear yourself or to subject them to experiences that were so painful and damaging for you.

It is clear in Josie's situation that someone is failing badly but, contrary to the common-sense assertion regularly heard that it is mothers like Josie who are failing their children, I would argue that it is Josie, Darren and Dean who are being failed. Josie's may sound like an extreme example, but over the 25 years I have been interviewing working-class parents and their children I have heard many desperate cases of families seeking help and failing to find it, or if they do eventually receive support, obtaining it only when the problems have become so entrenched that little can be done. Also, it was not just Josie who used a whole litany of negative words to describe both her own education and her experiences of her children's education. Working-class parents, in particular mothers, regularly used words such as horrible, humiliating, 'like a nightmare', scared, terrified, embarrassing and petrified when talking about past and present experiences of education. The very different levels of resources – material, social, but also psychological in terms of confidence and a sense of entitlement – add up to a substantial and unfair class difference.

Conclusion

Working-class children like Ricky and Shianne lack enriching and rewarding curriculum activities within schooling that draw on the strengths, and uphold the value, of their working-class cultures, while working-class mothers like Josie struggle without the support and encouragement to enable them to feel empowered in relation to their children's education. This is not just a result of narrow and overly prescriptive curricular content, and lack of affirmation for the working classes in the English educational system. Currently, if you are working class in England, and especially if you are poor, you are likely to have less-experienced and less-qualified teachers than more privileged students have,[19] as well as poorer educational facilities more generally.[20] In fairer and higher-achieving state educational systems such as those in Canada, Japan and Finland, children like Darren who are falling behind would receive extra support and more small-group input to enable them to catch up.[21] Perversely, in the English educational system it is the white middle-class children with assertive parents who are more likely to receive extra help and additional resources; they are more likely to be attending the better-resourced state schools, to be in smaller classes and to have parents with the confidence to make demands on the system. It is unsurprising, then, that socioeconomic attainment gaps widen, rather than narrow, as children progress through school,[22] implying that schooling exacerbates, rather than mitigates, social class inequalities in attainment outcomes. This may be how the English educational system has always worked, but that does not stop its being profoundly unjust. In the next chapter, I explore in greater depth how working-class children respond to and make sense of the everyday injustices they encounter in schooling.

FOUR

Class in the classroom

Introduction

> The school system increasingly seems like a mirage,
> the source of an immense, collective disappointment,
> a promised land which, like the horizon, recedes as
> one moves towards it.[1]

Building on the empirical case studies drawn on in the last
chapter, this chapter explores in more depth how the working
classes deal with the constant spectre of failure and the elusiveness
of success that they encounter daily in schooling. They also
increasingly have to deal with a lack of recognition, both as
successful learners and as valuable individuals, so a key question
this chapter engages with is 'How do the working classes
experience a relative educational failure that has come to be
seen as "a personal lack"?' These working-class dilemmas will
be explored through empirical case studies. The case studies
focus on interviews with working-class young people about their
experiences of being in the bottom set, as well as those young
people whose only educational option is low-status, inner-city
comprehensives seen by both themselves and others as demonised
and pathologised educational places.

I was struck by an assertion made by one of the respondents
in the Great British Class Survey, a survey of social class in the
United Kingdom carried out by Mike Savage and his colleagues
at the University of Manchester in 2013.[2] A male professor
commented that he would prefer to think of people for their

inherent value rather than their class. But the problem in England is that the question of an individual's inherent value can never be disentangled from their class position. This differential valuing of the upper, middle and working classes not only infuses the educational system, but has shaped its structure, influenced its practices and dictated the very different relationships that different social classes have to the system. Despite an expectation that the working classes should have the same relationship to state education as the middle classes, unsurprisingly – in view of the history of state schooling – they do not. As Andy Green shows, the history of working-class education has been one of control and cultural domination.[3] It would be hard to portray working-class experiences in education as generally fulfilling, as being about 'bettering oneself' in the classic middle-class mode. The working-class experience of education has traditionally been one of educational failure, not success. Central to working-class relationships to state schooling is that it is not *their* educational system. The system does not belong to them in the ways that it does to the middle classes, and they have little sense of belonging within it. As a consequence, aspects of education appear pointless and irrelevant, and there is extensive research documenting, in particular, white, working-class boys' sense of futility in relation to formal, school-based learning.[4] In place of middle-class enthusiasm for school-based learning there are more often a pragmatism, and strong remnants of historically rooted attitudes to education that recognise at an important level that the educational system is not theirs, does not work in their interests and considers them and their cultural knowledge as inferior.

This systematic denigration of working-class knowledge has a long history that dates from the establishment of state schooling in the 1870s through to the present. Micky Flanagan, in his BBC Radio 4 programme on social class,[5] discussed with his old school friends his experiences of being a pupil at an East End working-class comprehensive school in the 1970s. He joked that they had all left school with nothing, adding that he got to make an ash tray in the second year and then a bottle opener in the third year. Micky and his mates reminisced about Barry, who was the most ambitious kid in the class because he wanted to be a van driver. Flanagan told how the whole class had erupted in laughter at Barry the dreamer because no one in their school ever got to drive a van. What they did get to do was carry the stuff from the market to the van, but never to actually drive the van. He concluded that for him and his mates school and educational qualifications just seemed totally pointless.

The invidious consequences of being in the bottom sets

This sense of futility and worthlessness often runs very deep. In my research in English schools over a period of 25 years, working-class children have often said that they feel stupid, rubbish, 'no good', or even that they 'count for nothing' in the school context. For working-class children, classrooms are often places of routine everyday humiliations and slights. And those working-class children who become disaffected with school develop strong resentments about mistreatment and what they saw as unfairness. In the interviews that I conducted their words were often infused with a sense of the righteous indignation that once underpinned a strong working-class politics. In the absence of that righteous indignation more generally there has been a re-emergence of a class cultural oppression characterised by a middle-class horror at the sight of poverty, and the ridiculing of the white working-classes through portrayals of 'chav' culture. Working-class children, across race and gender, frequently talk about feeling a powerful sense of injustice about the way they are seen and treated. Such factors are at the heart of the social divide in educational outcomes. Psychological research shows overwhelmingly that performance and behaviour in an educational context can be profoundly influenced by the way we feel that we are seen and judged by others. When we expect to be viewed as inferior our abilities seem to be diminished, and this sense of inferiority is particularly strong in the bottom sets. As part of a recent research study I spent time interviewing and talking with bottom-set students in an English comprehensive school. Their sense of abjection and failure was palpable:

Satvinder: *Right now, because I'm in the bottom set for everything I don't like it, because I'm only doing the foundation paper, and*

I don't ... I really don't want to do that. Because from Year 6 when I left I went I'm going to put my head down, and do my work, but I never did. And then it ... like, every year I say it, but I never do it. [...] I haven't even done it this year either. [...] Yeah, I could have, like, gone to a better higher place, and then I could have done everything I was hoping to.

Diane: *And now?*

Satvinder: *There is no hope.*

Atik: *I think I failed proper badly in the tests and that's why I'm in a proper bad set now ... I can just answer the questions really easy because there's like no really smart people and they behave quite bad as well and they influence me ... So I've just become rubbish.*

Joe: *The behaviour's bad. You don't learn unless you're in the first set.*

Shulah: *The behaviour, it gets worse in the bottom set when, like, teachers don't pay attention to you. And they pay attention to, like, the higher ability students and, like, you get bored because there's nothing for you to do if you don't understand the work.*

In all four quotes, low sets are clearly perceived to be places of educational failure and despair, where children are written off and have no hope of succeeding. This is not what any parent would want for their child, nor what any teacher should want for their students. Yet, over the 25 years that I have been researching in schools children in bottom sets have regularly described themselves as stupid, useless and rubbish.

Even starker was the collective view of a group of white, working-class boys in the bottom set, who felt that school had nothing to offer them:

Diane: *If you had a choice what would you choose to learn?*

Jason: *Nothing.*

George: *Nothing.*

Andy: *No idea.*

Paul: *Definitely nothing!*

Here we see how destructive the educational system is for those who struggle, swallowed up in a remorseless system of hierarchical ranking and a competitive counting culture. We can see the consequences for the individual in Jason's poignant advocacy for children like himself:

> *Some kids they just can't do it, like they find the work too hard, or they can't concentrate because too much is going on for them. Then they are put like as rubbish learners and put in the bottom set, and no one cares about them even though they are the ones who need the most help. They should be getting the most help.*

There are strong resonances here with Josie's passionate plea for more help in the last chapter.

So far I have drawn on the voices of secondary school students, but there are growing practices of setting and streaming in primary schools. This is a six-year-old in a London primary school:

> *They [the Lions] think they are better than us. They think they are good at every single thing and the second group, Tigers, there are some people that think they are good and more important than us. And one of the boys in Giraffes he was horrible to me and he said "get lost slow tortoise" but my group are Monkeys and we are only second to bottom.*

At a recent conference a researcher spoke with a mixture of horror and disbelief as he recounted going into a primary classroom where there were four ability groups – flying squirrels, tree squirrels, ground squirrels, and a bottom set called marmots because they are a type of squirrel that lives under the ground.

What concerned me, in addition to their feelings of futility, unfairness and humiliation, was that, unlike the top sets – which were predominantly white and middle class – all the lower-set students were working class and ethnically diverse. These young people may express a strong sense of individual failure but they simultaneously share a collective class fate. The young people I met have little opportunity for finding self-fulfilment and realising their potential through schooling. Schooling should be about establishing 'a community of learners', but setting and streaming on the basis of perceived ability destroys any sense of community. It also widens the class attainment gap as middle-class children in the top sets benefit while working-class children, disproportionately placed in lower sets and streams, are further disadvantaged.[6]

Working-class responses to the educational system are in large measure a reaction to the attitudes and actions of those with more power and agency to effect policies and practices within schooling. These include not only teachers but, more influentially, the middle-class majority, policy makers and politicians. In a research project investigating the extent to which children felt included in schooling, secondary school students were asked whether they felt that they had the confidence to act within schooling; whether they felt they belonged, as individuals and as groups, within the school community; and whether they felt that they had the power to influence the procedures and practices that shaped their learning.[7] The vast majority of the working-class students talked about a sense of powerlessness and educational worthlessness, and feelings that they were not really valued and respected within education. But it was working-class boys, in particular, who expressed anger at the way they were treated.

Danny: *Some teachers are a bit snobby, sort of. And some teachers act as if the child is stupid. Because they've got a posh accent. Like they talk without "innits" and "mans", like they talk proper English. And they say, "That isn't the way you talk" – like putting you down. Like I think telling you a different way is sort of good, but I think the way they do it isn't good because they correct you and make you look stupid.*

Martin: *Those teachers look down on you.*

In both Danny's and Martin's words we can see how educational processes are, simultaneously, classed processes in which relations of teaching and learning too often position working-class pupils as inadequate learners with inadequate cultural backgrounds, looked down on for their 'stupidity'. I suggest that it is not insignificant that their teacher with 'the posh accent' who 'looks down on them' is an Oxbridge graduate just one year out of teacher training. Many of Danny and Martin's teachers were similarly young and inexperienced. As Danny told me in a later interview, "who is he to look down on me, he's just a kid". Of course, schools benefit from a mix of new and experienced teachers, but Danny and Martin's inner-city comprehensive had far more of the former than the latter when it would have benefited from a mix of both.

Educational processes in the classroom are rarely uniform and clearly do not affect all working-class students in the same ways. Class is always, to varying degrees, mediated by gender and race, and, as I will examine in more detail later, the roots and consequences of alienation from schooling differ according to ethnicity. What were present, though, for all the working-class students in the study, were varying degrees of alienation. As the extract below shows, black, working-class girls can feel just as marginalised and alienated by schooling as are white, working-class boys.

Sharmaine: *Sometimes we feel left out.*

Sarah: *Because you know, teachers are not meant to have favourites.*

Sharmaine: *You can have, but you can't show it, you know. That's unfair to the other people.*

Sarah: *Because there's a whole class there and you want to pick that particular person, and you are nice to that one, and the rest you don't care about.*

Alex: *But everyone has to be the same.*

Sharmaine: *He needs to treat everyone equal.*

Reduced to a number: the impact of excessive testing and assessment on learner identities

We can see in what both working-class boys and girls say across ethnic difference some of the hidden injuries of class that are enshrined and perpetuated through educational policies and practices. These injuries of class are particularly raw and vivid in relation to the growing processes of assessment and testing in schools. England is now the most tested nation in the world.[8] I first became concerned about the effect of SATs (standardised assessment tasks) in primary schools at the turn of the 21st century.[9] Below are some quotes from the 40 children aged 10 and 11 whom I interviewed. From visiting primary schools and observing in classrooms, I could see that the SATs were shifting children's identifications as learners; many, particularly the girls and the working-class children, were expressing much anxiety and a lack of confidence in themselves as learners.

> Hannah: *I'm really scared about the SATs. Mrs O'Brien [a teacher at the school] came and talked to us about our spelling and I'm no good at spelling and David [the class teacher] is giving us times tables tests every morning and I'm hopeless at times tables so I'm frightened I'll do the SATs and I'll be a nothing.*
>
> Diane: *I don't understand, Hannah. You can't be a nothing.*
>
> Hannah: *Yes, you can cos you have to get a level like a level 4 or a level 5 and if you're no good at spellings and times tables you don't get those levels and so you're a nothing.*
>
> Diane: *I'm sure that's not right.*
>
> Hannah: *Yes it is cos that's what Mrs O'Brien was saying.*

This is a particularly stark example but it exemplifies some of the ways in which children's identifications as learners are constructed through the assessment process. For Hannah, what constitutes academic success is correct spelling and knowing your times tables. She is an accomplished writer, a gifted dancer and artist and good at problem solving, yet none of those skills make her somebody in her own eyes. Instead she constructs herself as a failure, an academic non-person, by a metonymic shift in which she comes to see herself entirely in terms of the level to which her performance in the SATs is ascribed. Although the school had a general policy of playing down the importance of SATs, Hannah's teacher, who was in his second year of teaching, was still feeling under intense external pressure to ensure that his pupils did well. As is apparent in the following quotation, the fever pitch in the classroom surrounding the impending SATs was generated in no small part by his anxieties.

> *I was appalled by how most of you did on the science test: You don't know anything. I want to say that you are judged at the end of the day by what you get in the SATs and some of you won't even get level 2.*

Some children resisted and challenged such all-embracing judgements; for example, Terry was outraged by his teacher's comment and shouted out, "Hold on we're not that bad!" However, others, like Hannah, appeared to accept and internalise his criticisms. Hannah's account underscores the extent to which SATs have set in motion a new set of tensions with which Year 6 students are expected to cope. As the quotations presented later indicate, all the children, apart from Terry, expressed varying degrees of anxiety about failure. While there is a gender dimension to this anxiety, in that girls expressed higher degrees of anxiety than boys, the overall impression from the Year 6 interviews was that most pupils of both sexes took the SATs very seriously. They wanted to do well. At the same time, children expressed a great deal of concern about the narrow focus of the SATs and not being able to produce their best under strict (and unfamiliar) test conditions. Their concerns seem to be borne out by research into the validity of the Key Stage 2 English SATs:

> Nicely rounded handwriting and reasonable spelling
> of fairly simple words seemed to impress some

markers favourably. In contrast, idiosyncratic or jerky handwriting with insecure spellings seemed to prejudice some markers against the content.[10]

The students also seemed very aware of the (not so) hidden agenda surrounding SATs:

Mary: *SATs are about how good the teachers have been teaching you and if everybody gets really low marks they think the teachers haven't been teaching you properly.*

Diane: *So what are the SATs for?*

Jackie: *To see if the teachers have taught us anything.*

Terry: *If we don't know nothing then the teacher will get all the blame.*

Jackie: *Yeah. It's the teacher's fault.*

Tunde: *Yeah. They get blamed.*

Yet, despite frequent rationalisations that SATs were primarily judgements of teaching, nearly all the children indicated a sense of unease and feelings of discomfort about what SATs might reveal about themselves as learners. The working-class children, in particular, seemed to be indicating far-reaching consequences in which good SATs results were linked to positive life prospects and, concomitantly, poor results meant future failures and hardships.

Sharon: *I think I'll get a 2, only Stuart will get a 6.*

Diane: *So if Stuart gets a 6 what will that say about him?*

Sharon: *He's heading for a good job and a good life and it shows he's not gonna be living on the streets and stuff like that.*

Diane: *And if you get a level 2 what will that say about you?*

Sharon: *Um, I might not have a good life in front of me and I might grow up and do something naughty or something like that.*

In three of the focus group sessions the children drew on an apocalyptic tale of "the boy who ruined his chances". The following excerpt is from the girls' focus group, but both the boys' and the mixed group referred to the same example in order to exemplify how things can go terribly wrong in the SATs if you don't make the right choices.

Norma: *There was someone so good at writing stories …*

Mary: *Yeah, and he wrote a leaflet …*

Norma: *He picked to write a leaflet and then when he wrote the leaflet he blew it.*

Lily: *He just ruined his whole SAT. He ruined it. If he'd written the story he would have got a really good mark. He was the best at writing stories. And he thought he wanted to try it out … and he just ruined it for himself.*

Norma: *Mrs O'Brien said that he was … what was the word, kind of scared thing …?*

Diane: *Got in a panic.*

Norma: *Yeah, and he didn't do the story because he thought he would get that wrong.*

Mary: *So he did the leaflet and he just ruined his chances, totally ruined his chances.*

In this excerpt and the others, performance in SATs was about far more than simply getting a test right or wrong, it was conflated in the children's minds with future prospects. To perform badly is to 'ruin one's chances'. At other times there was more disputation and contention about the importance of SATs for future prospects:

Diane: *So are they important, SATs?*

Lily: *Depends.*

Tunde: *Yes.*

Terry: *No, definitely not.*

Lewis: *It does affect your life.*

Ayse: *Yeah, it does affect your life.*

Terry: *No, as if it means, you know, I do badly then that means I'm gonna be a road sweeper.*

However, while Terry is clear that SATs have no impact on future prospects, other students lack his certainty:

Diane: *You mean, you think that if you do badly in SATs then you won't be able to do well or get good jobs?*

Jackie: *Yeah, cos that's what David's saying.*

Diane: *What is he saying?*

Jackie: *He's saying if we don't like, get good things, in our SATS, when we grow up we are not gonna get good jobs and …*

Ricky: *Be plumbers and road-sweepers …*

Tunde: *But what if you wanted to do that?*

Diane: *Instead of what?*

Ricky: *Footballers, singers, vets, archaeologists. We ain't gonna be nothing like that if we don't get high levels.*

Diane: *And does that worry you about your future?*

Jackie: *Yeah.*

Lewis: *Yeah.*

Since then, the focus on assessment and testing has grown apace, undermining the well-being and morale of not only students but their teachers as well. One of the most powerful illustrations of the latter was an open letter written by a teacher to Nicky Morgan, at that time Secretary of Education, that was published in the *New Statesman*.[11] The teacher reflected that:

> In some ways I don't feel like a teacher at all any more. I prepare children for tests and, if I'm honest, I do it quite well. It's not something I'm particularly proud of as it's not as if it provided my class with any transferable, real life skills during the process. They've not enjoyed it, I've not enjoyed it but we've done it: and one thing my children know how to do is answer test questions. They've written raps about how to answer test questions, they've practised test questions at home and test questions in school, they've had extra tuition to help them understand the test questions. They can do test questions – they just haven't had time to do anything else ... worse than being a teacher in this system is being a child at the mercy of it.

In 2016 an NUT survey on primary assessment found that 97% of teachers agreed or strongly agreed that the SATs had had a negative impact on children's access to a broad and balanced curriculum.[12] They also wrote of demoralisation, demotivation and physical and mental distress. The following are just two of many quotes from the survey indicating the negative consequences for both children's well-being and their sense of themselves as learners.

> We have had a massive increase in social, emotional and mental health issues this year. It has been reported that teachers and schools are to blame for this, but

we have not designed a curriculum and testing for which most of our children are not emotionally or developmentally ready for. Our children are being set up to fail! Ministers don't seem to realise that there are children at the end of these tests. They are only concerned with measuring teacher accountability.

Many of the children who previously enjoyed school now detest education. This is a crime and a shame because, in its incompetence, the Government is willingly and knowingly making children hate learning with a passion, rather than harbour an environment of lifelong learning.[13]

Dealing with the damaging experience of attending demonised schools

In the UK a market–driven, privatised educational system that operates with a crude, test–led system of attributing value has resulted in the devaluation and pathologisation of many working-class students, particularly those who are not predicted five or more A*–C results in the national GCSE exams taken at age 15/16. It has also resulted in the devaluing and demonisation of the schools, mostly comprehensives, that these working-class students attend. We do not need to scrutinise research reports in order to recognise the low esteem and contempt with which such schools and their pupils are widely regarded. Reading the national and local press, and also spending any concerted time with groups of middle-class parents, will reveal a litany of failures and lacks in which words like 'rubbish', 'bad', 'sink' and 'rough' proliferate. Much has been written about middle-class choice making, including middle-class strategies of avoiding so–called 'sink' schools; but there is far less work on the repercussions for working-class students of this stigmatisation of themselves and the schools they attend. They automatically become the losers in an increasingly competitive educational game.

The growing processes of polarisation and segregation, caused largely by middle-class parental choice, are fuelling early school leaving by positioning working-class students in demonised and stigmatised educational places. In the following two quotes we can see the negative repercussions for working-class learner identities.

> *And I've been hearing that if you don't get into any of the good schools they send you to one of the rubbish schools. In school I've been hearing everyone saying "I hope I don't go to Chiltern" and stuff like that. So I then thought that was really awful because all the kids there are bad and no good at learning.* (George, White English, working class)

> *Deerpark is still going to be rubbish when it's changed ... because there are still the same students and the students are crap.* (Teyfik, Turkish, working class)

But George ends up at Chiltern, while Teyfik goes to Deerpark, and both have to manage the balance between going to schools seen to be 'rubbish with crap students' and trying to be successful learners. However, such processes of segregation are having a wider effect beyond their negative impact on individual children. They are changing and limiting the ways in which the different social classes relate to each other, and this is explored further in Chapter Six.

I am now going to concentrate on the secondary school experience of four students whom I interviewed who had all been in the same class at Beckwith, a multi-ethnic, working-class, inner-city primary school. Mustafa, Kirsty, Jordan and Lindsey all went on to one of the six demonised secondary schools in our study. Lindsey went to Phoenix, and Mustafa, Kirsty and Jordan all went to Chiltern. Lindsey was White English, working class and Mustafa was an African refugee from a middle-class background but whose parents were now unemployed. Both Kirsty and Jordan were mixed race and working class. (Kirsty has a Black British father and a White English mother, while Jordan's mother is Trinidadian and his father is Irish). Lindsey and Jordan lived in lone-mother families, while Kirsty and Mustafa lived with both parents. All these children were interviewed three times over the course of their first year at secondary school. Lindsey and Jordan were also interviewed in the first term of their second year. Parents (all mothers) were interviewed once, as were the year tutors in the two schools. Lindsey and Mustafa lived on the same large, 'sink' council estate. Kirsty and Jordan both lived on a smaller, low-rise council estate that was viewed as slightly less 'rough' than the sprawling, high-rise estate the other two children occupied. Of the four children, only Lindsey has chosen the secondary school that she attends.

When Kirsty found out that she had failed to get into Nelson Mandela and had been offered a place at Chiltern, a school she had earlier described "as total rubbish", her mother told me "she burst into tears and ran into her bedroom and just sobbed and sobbed". Mustafa, who had also chosen Nelson Mandela as his first choice, on finding out he had to go to Chiltern, tried to creatively reinvent it as a school offering the prospect of improvement. He said, "My dad says schools go up and down and Chiltern's near the bottom now so it can only go up. When I go there I think its results are gonna go up."

Jordan created a typology of schools. Nelson Mandela, his choice, was "a mix of posh kids, computer whizzes, people who like to learn and some rough kids and just a few tough kids". Phoenix had "a few poshies and laid backs, quite a few toughs and some roughs but mostly kids who need help with their learning". Lawrence Grove had "no poshies, a few toughs, quite a few learners and some laid backs who just can't be bothered". Chiltern, the school Jordan ended up going to, had "a mix of rough kids, tough kids and just a few poshies but not many that want to learn". Sutton Boys, which he described as "well horrible", had "mostly got tough kids and rough kids". However, when I asked him what was the right mix for him he generated a student composition that was not available in any of the local secondary schools. He wanted to be in a school "with mostly learners and just a few rough kids and poshies and no tough kids at all because otherwise you do rubbish at school and you can't get on later when you're more grown up".

Jordan's typology bears further scrutiny. Class and gender are implicit in his categorisations. The poshies are those middle-class children who display rather than hide their cultural and social advantage, computer whizzes cross class boundaries but are a male grouping, as are the tough kids who raise the troubling spectre of bullying. Rough kids are the working-class equivalent of the poshies. In failing to hide the markings of poverty, they are often reduced in the children's peer group conversations to "tramps".

Lindsey chose a school so full of rough and tough kids that the local authority had closed it down, reopening it in a new guise. It was this 'fresh start' that attracted Lindsey, who asserted, "It's a totally new school now, different from the old one. That was a bad one, this is going to be a good one."

So how did these four children, with their range of very different responses to the prospect of moving on to secondary school, deal with such invidious judgements of the schools they were going to. How did they variously manage schooling that "was bad but is now good", "'total rubbish", "full of tramps", "one of the worst schools but on the way up" or Jordan's slightly more nuanced "has a mix of rough kids, tough kids and just a few poshies but not many that want to learn"?

As Jordan made clear, "the toughs" were in a minority in all the schools he characterised. Yet, the prevailing representation of all these schools, apart from Nelson Mandela, was that they were overwhelmed with bullying, gang warfare and ill-disciplined, disruptive pupils. As Goffman asserts, to be 'with' a particular group, in this case the 'rough' children who attend demonised schools, often leads to the assumption that one is what the others are.[14] Yet, as the children's words illustrate, their actual experience of attending such schools was far more multifaceted, stressing difference rather than sameness.

Surprisingly, the most creative reinvention and generative resistance to the negative representations of these schools came from Lindsey, who went to the most demonised of the two schools these children moved on to.

Phoenix, as a failing school, was deemed to be so bad that it was closed down and reopened with a new name and a new head teacher. Then he left suddenly and was replaced by another head, who also left after a term, to be replaced by yet another new head. So Lindsey had to deal with three head teachers in her first year. At the end of the summer term she commented wryly:

This new principal says the school's gonna evolve from what it is now. You know everything is gonna get better, change for the better. He's the third principal who's said that. It's been kind of difficult them changing because when I first came it was like the new school with him as principal. He was our new principal, kind of special and then we got a new principal, but now we've got a different principal and it's hard to change the picture because he's not the one you're expecting.

In contrast to the dominant representations of these inner-city schools that reduce the student body down into a common mass of 'rubbish', Lindsey's focus, like Jordan's, was on difference. She told me that her class was "a wide range of mixed people, like loud, shy, confident, unconfident, quiet but mostly loud". Her emphasis on difference allowed her a strategy of following her own, rather than others', leads:

Everyone's different so I just stick to my own behaviour because I don't like to copy other people's behaviour if they are too loud or a bit too quiet. Best to be just me.

When I asked Lindsey to describe the average child at Phoenix she not only resisted my attempts to impose uniformity but also began to deconstruct the category of 'rough'.

Diane: *So how would you describe the average child in your school?*

Lindsey: *A mixture of a lot of things, a bit loud but sometimes a bit quiet and successful, maybe, I hope.*

Diane: *Do you remember Jordan saying it had lots of rough kids?*

Lindsey: *Yes, but I don't think that's right because I'm not from a very good background because around my area there's always police up there and there's lots of violence and drugs but we've got a nice flat. We live in a block of flats that's very unhygienic and scruffy but inside we've got a nice flat so you can't say rough just from the outside.*

Here we have a reflexive understanding that disrupts dominant negative representations of inner-city schools and the predominantly working-class children who attend them. What Lindsey demonstrates is that to judge a school by superficial appearances is to overlook the complex diversity that characterises schools in areas with a multiplicity of ethnicities and myriad gradations of poverty and affluence jostling side by side. As Lindsey, and also Jordan, made clear, the result is complex differences and differentiations, not 'shit heaps' and 'rubbish dumps'. Jordan, Kirsty and Mustafa all went to the same inner-city comprehensive – one described in the national tabloid press shortly before they started as 'drug dealers' paradise' and 'riven with gang warfare'. This was very anxiety-inducing for the three of them and they talked about the 'threat' of drugs and drug dealers extensively in the earlier interviews. It was Mustafa who expressed these fears most succinctly:

> *It's seen as a druggie school. I seen it in the newspaper. There's these boys selling drugs and this little boy. They were asking him to buy drugs and stuff and he said no and the big kids got angry with the boy for not buying any drugs and they threatened him with a knife. There is no way I want that to happen to me.*

And:

> *I was asking my dad about it cos say one of my friends who goes to Chiltern with me and then when we become teenagers he decides to sell drugs what shall I do? And he said we'll talk about it if it happens but it worries me and I really wanted to know because I do have a big friend and he's my best friend at Chiltern and he might be older than me but I play with him and he protects me, but then say he starts drugs, then who will I go to?*

There is both a poignancy and an attempt to grapple with complex moral dilemmas in Mustafa's text, but underpinning both quotations is also an overriding sense of Chiltern as a risky, unsafe place to be. It is extremely difficult for children like Mustafa to challenge prevailing images of inner-city schooling and step outside the dominant representations of schools like

Chiltern. However, by the end of the year all three children had begun to challenge pervasive views that Chiltern was 'a rubbish school' by constructing a collage of good as well as bad aspects of the school.

Mustafa: *The most important thing for me for Year 8 is to get a good reputation.*

Diane: *Great. And what about your school, because before you came here you told me it had a bad reputation?*

Mustafa: *I don't think that's right any more because it's not all bad. It's got good things as well as bad things.*

Jordan: *My mum told me it was a bad school.*

Diane: *And what do you think now you've been here for a year?*

Jordan: *I think it's a good school most of the time. It's a bad school when there's a fight because everyone goes — "run for it". And everyone goes running to the fight. But the good thing about it is the education. The education is good.*

Diane: *So how do you feel about Chiltern now you've been here for a year?*

Kirsty: *I feel quite alright now and it's not too bad. Like the kids, we all get along nice and the teachers are quite friendly.*

Diane: *You said before you came it was full of bad kids.*

Kirsty: *(laughing) No, there's quite a few good kids and lots in between. I don't want to move school any more.*

From what these children say it is apparent that experiences of going to demonised schools are messy and complicated rather than uniform. All four are attempting to construct different visions of their schools to the prevailing ones. They are challenging the dominant views of their schools. At the same time there is no getting away from the consequences, both educational and emotional, of being positioned at the bottom of the secondary schools market. While we can see in their narratives a compelling drive to make good what is often depicted as uniformly bad, these children are still the losers in the educational game. Perhaps the most unjust consequence is that, despite this considerable positive energy towards construction and creation, it is so much harder for them to translate more than a fraction of their creativity into the kind of educational achievement that is valued within the current educational system.

Despite sterling efforts to make the most of a difficult fate, at one level all the working-class children recognise, like Michael below, that going to schools seen to be 'rubbish' leads to 'rubbish opportunities'. As the next quote shows, the significance of being in low-attaining schools is not lost on working-class children.

> Michael: *I won't get in to Westbury so I'll have to go to Sutton. There's only one really bad thing about going to Sutton.*

> Diane: *What?*

> Michael: *I ain't gonna be a vet if I go there.*

> Diane: *Why do you think you won't be a vet if you go to Sutton?*

> Michael: *Well, everyone says you can't get a good education there and you need a good education to be a vet.*

In a research project I was involved in, conducted from 2010 to 2012, the constraints and difficulties surrounding working-class educational experiences were ever present. The research took place in a large, multi-ethnic, predominantly working-class comprehensive school in a town in south-east England and focused specifically on working-class young people at risk of educational failure – those whom the school identified as the most likely to 'drop out'. The data comprised five focus group interviews (each with between 8 and 12 young people) and repeat in-depth interviews with 12 students aged 14 and 15. The students were unambiguously working class. None had parents who had been to university. Two of the young people lived in lone-parent households dependent on benefits, and one young man was looked after by the local authority. Other young people lived in families with fathers working in jobs such as security guard, taxi driver, builder and car-paint sprayer. Six of the 12 were in receipt of FSM and a further young woman was eligible but had not claimed her entitlement.

These young people, despite being disadvantaged, were good neoliberal subjects, buying heavily into processes of individualisation and free choice. Unlike young working-class people in the 1960s, 1970s and 1980s, for whom early school leaving was often not seen as a personal failure, these young people had high aspirations that were in conflict with their actual labour market possibilities. They also expressed a strong sense of individual responsibility for their learning and, in particular, their failure to achieve educational success. Students told us "it's down to the individual how well you do at school", "you have to make yourself stand out compared to all the other people doing the same exams", and "if you want to do well you just have to work really hard. You can't blame the school or your teachers." These young people were heavily invested in notions of the autonomous, self-reliant individual responsible for any future outcomes; we glimpse the ways in which symbolic domination works by making the individual responsible for their own success or failure, rather than recognising that some things are just not possible if you have virtually none of the necessary resources.

It is unsurprising that their strong sense of individual responsibility for learning was coupled with weak, often disengaged, learner identities. A lot of the time they failed to see the relevance of, in particular, the academic subjects they were studying. As Yussif said, "I think GCSEs, the only reason we do them is so we can get into college." There was a strong sense that education is not really for 'people like them'; that they weren't the right sort of people for academic learning. The constraints and difficulties surrounding working-class educational experiences were ever present, evident in the students' lack of enthusiasm for school-based learning. As Jerome told us, "I just want to get school over and done with", while Carly said, "I feel like I just want to go home, as soon as the bell goes, I just wanna go home". For most of the students most of the time, school-based learning singularly failed to inspire and enthuse.

A majority of the young people specified that the most enjoyable thing about school was being with friends, rather than any aspect of learning. So, when Shula was asked what she most enjoyed about school she responded "my friends", Husnara commented, "the best thing about coming to school is meeting my friends", and Yussif asserted, "you need friends because it is just so crap, really boring and stuff". While they recognised that qualifications were key to "a good job and a good life", in place of active engagement with learning was a sense that schooling was something to be got through rather than enjoyed. Here again it is vital to acknowledge the importance of history and the wider context for this sense of having a spoilt learner identity: the dominant discourses that constitute the working-class as inadequate, failing learners seem to have changed little over the last 150 years. It is unsurprising, then, that working-class students continue to fail to see the relevance of many of the academic subjects they are studying.

Conclusion

In this chapter I have looked at how the working classes deal with the constant spectre of failure and the elusiveness of success that they encounter daily in schooling. England is unique in using testing to control what is taught in schools, to monitor teaching standards and to encourage parents to choose schools based on the test results – all to the damage of children's well-being.[15] There is plenty of contemporary evidence of the damage wreaked by competitive individualism, constant assessment and testing and placement in bottom sets. In UNICEF's report in 2007 on those aspects of children's well-being attributable to how well they are served by their national educational systems, the UK languished near the bottom with an overall score of 90, well below the average for the 24 countries surveyed.[16] So, for example, the proportion of young people not looking beyond low-skilled work was more than 35%. Even more concerning, only slightly more than 40% found their peers kind and helpful, in contrast to most other European countries, including Finland,

Norway, Denmark and Sweden, where over 70% found their peers kind and helpful. Less than 20% of UK pupils liked school a lot. Just as concerning, in relation to self-harming and risk behaviours, the UK languishes at the very bottom of the rankings by a considerable distance.

Overall, the UNICEF report concludes that, in terms of both children's subjective sense of well-being and objective criteria, the UK is markedly below the average. We are seeing the lowest levels of children's well-being in the UK in decades. As research by Ipsos MORI in 2011 that investigated the underlying processes driving low well-being in the UK concluded, children are less happy and satisfied with their lives than are children in a majority of other countries because of the far higher levels of materialism, accompanied by intense competitiveness and individualism, to be found in contemporary British society.[17] There is a pressing need to re-centre care, collaboration and empathy in our schools. The *Good Childhood Report* published by The Children's Society in 2015 found that 'overall children in England have relatively low levels of subjective well-being compared to other countries. England ranked 13th out of 14 countries for life satisfaction and 11th for feelings of happiness, and feeling positive about the future. This is despite being one of the wealthiest countries in the survey.'[18]

Current research places the UK 19th out of 20 countries in a survey of well-being, with young people aged 15–21 in the UK lagging behind young people in France and Germany, as well as those in countries such as Israel, Turkey, Russia and China.[19] But, while levels of educational well-being generally are low in England, research also shows that low achievers have lower levels of well-being than high achievers.[20] It is the working-class children clustered in the lower sets who are suffering the most. But working-class children are also clustered disproportionately in schools seen to be underperforming. These happen to be the schools with younger, more inexperienced teachers who stay for relatively short periods of time. They also tend to be the schools with the most intense focus on 'teaching to the test', as well as often having less-advantageous funding levels than schools with more middle-class intakes. In the next chapter I turn to a very different group of working-class children and young people –

the small minority who are seen to be educational successes
rather than failures.

FIVE

Social mobility:
a problematic solution

Introduction

So far this book has focused on the majority of the working classes who are set up to fail in English education. This chapter focuses on the minority who are seen to succeed academically, the working classes who are socially mobile through education. In doing so it attempts to unpick the challenges in putting clever and working class together (as opposed to the endlessly bright middle and upper classes). The chapter also engages with the painful compromises that can arise if you are working class and educationally successful.

Social mobility has an iconic place in English political discourse. It appears as if the less mobility there is, the more it becomes a preoccupation of politicians and policy makers. It is nearly always seen in straightforwardly positive ways, particularly within political, policy and media discourses. In contrast, this chapter argues that it constitutes a problematic solution to educational inequalities where the negatives have consistently threatened to undermine the positives. In the first part of the chapter these problematic aspects are explored in the 1950s and 1960s, the period in which I was growing up and the time that Jackson and Marsden were writing about; I then draw on case studies relating to the 1980s and the more recent period of my own research.

The 21st century has seen an opening up of new educational horizons for the educationally successful working-class. Yet, at the same time, social mobility is a process that is constantly troubled by questions of differential values and valuing. It is also one in which the working classes are seriously disadvantaged by their lack of access to privileged social networks. Recent governments, Labour, Conservative and Coalition, have viewed creating aspiring students as more effective, and clearly cheaper, than putting money into education. Yet again, as I have argued in earlier chapters, this constitutes a policy approach that makes the working classes responsible for their own educational success without providing them with the resources to make that success possible.

The second part of the chapter unpicks the assumption that more working-class young people going to university is an unmitigated success, and examines the extent to which a working-class student's degree has the same value as a middle- or upper-class student's degree in the 21st century. It also explores how the working-class university student manages the difficulties of reconciling a working-class background with the middle-class environment of the university when one class culture is seen to have less value than another.

At the collective level, social mobility is no solution to either educational inequalities or wider social and economic injustices. But at the individual level it is also an inadequate solution, particularly for those of us whose social mobility was driven by a desire 'to put things right' and 'make things better' for the communities we came from and the people we left behind.[1] In earlier work I have argued that social mobility is a form of cruel optimism: it is powerfully desired but, in reality, is often a barrier to thriving.[2] So many of us from working-class backgrounds invest heavily in the fantasy that our relentless efforts will bring us love, care, intimacy, success, security and well-being, even when they are highly unlikely to do so because, in doing so, we are forming optimistic attachments to the very power structures that have oppressed us, and our families before us. Social mobility is one such optimistic fantasy that ensnares and works on both the individual psyche and the collective consciousness. It has become the preferred cure for social problems and educational inequalities, promoted by politicians on both the Right and Left. But in deeply unequal societies like England it has come to feel much more like a social ill, one that harms both the socially mobile individual and the communities they grew up in.

Struggling up ladders, falling down snakes

Although, for the most part, Jackson and Marsden told a positive story of advancement and working-class educational success, they also wrote eloquently of a handful of working-class boys who made it to Oxbridge, and it is in their account of these experiences that we really glimpse the psychological costs involved. They describe a group of nine working-class boys who, in aiming for Oxbridge, appeared like Icarus to fly too high. Seven of the nine took thirds or lower seconds. The plummeting of academic results in the Oxbridge group was seen by Jackson and Marsden as an indicator of the waves of disturbance across much of the sample. They noted that 'this small group seem to be sensitively recording a crumbling away' that was felt through much of their wider sample.[3] A number reflected on 'what was it all for' – a question that Jackson and Marsden argue was 'born of the difficult and the obscure social rifts and struggles which for them had become part of the process of education itself'.[4] Jackson and Marsden question whether these young men did want to move forward as successful, middle-class individuals, or whether, in some way, they wanted to hold on to their backgrounds. They write about an endemic 'lost feeling for source, means, purpose; a loss heightened by an absence of the sustaining powers of social and family relationships'.

> There is something infinitely pathetic in these former working-class children who lost their roots young, and now with their rigid middle class accent preserve 'the stability of all our institutions temporal and spiritual by avariciously reading the lives of 'Top People', or covet the private schools, and glancing back at the society from which they came see no more there than the 'dim' or the 'specimens'.[5]

Their stark message was that social mobility is not a positive process if it is accompanied by snobbery, shame and ultra-conformity. This message was reinforced by Dennis Marsden's account of his own Oxbridge experience:

> I found quickly that entry to Cambridge was not so easy. Unfortunately I found less quickly that entry to that Cambridge wasn't necessary or even important. That Cambridge, the Cambridge of the toffs was there alright, but it remained supremely indifferent to my existence.[6]

He went on to explain: 'I didn't make many friends. I was snubbed in the cruising club – and heavily patronised by the club steward there who soon saw I wasn't like the other gentlemen. I had to wait three years for admission to the swimming club.' His rather depressing conclusion was that 'from being at school one of nature's chosen few I had become overnight at Cambridge a C-streamer'.

Melvin Bragg's reflections on his social mobility are both poignant and wistful:

> We were working class, and you don't lose that. Later on, I bolted on middle classness but I think the working-class thing hasn't gone away and it never will go away. I don't want it to go away. I don't try to make it go away. Quite a few of my interactions and responses are still the responses I had when I was 18 or 19. And the other things are bolted on and it is a mix. It is what it is, and a lot of people are like that. I'm a class mongrel.[7]

Bragg goes on to talk about his adolescent years, a period when he was doing extremely well academically but one that was also torn by fears and anxieties. He reflects that 'I think it's left scars of nervousness that I have still. I'm just very nervous a lot of the time.' His words are both poignant and painful. Middle-classness has been 'bolted on', it is neither integrated nor natural. Rather, it sounds like an artificial appendage, and as if there is an element of enforcement; it has been a brutal process, as he reveals when describing his two episodes of mental breakdown. We see how he has been wounded by the process of social mobility. Despite his fame and ennoblement (he is now Lord Bragg), he still carries a sense of being a social perversion – a class mongrel. And, as his words illustrate, there was a powerful desire to hold on to a working-class past even as he moved up the social ladder.

So far, these have all been men's tales, but in the next section I outline two incidents from my own social mobility journey in order to provide a female perspective and to start to sketch out a genealogy of social mobility that underlines the messiness of social mobility journeys and how they can be about tumbling down even as you climb up. This first episode, from my first day at school, signifies the beginning of my social mobility journey – the awakening of a powerful yearning for something I was not seen to be entitled to.

I want you to picture a scene in a small-town primary school on the edge of the coalfields in Derbyshire in the mid-1950s. A little girl of barely five years has been gently pushed through the school gate by a harassed mother with baby in pram, a two-year-old plonked on top and a crying three-year-old clutching the bar at the side of the pram. The mother rushes off. The little girl is already late and it is her first day at school. She cautiously makes her way to the front entrance and a kindly secretary ushers her into the reception classroom. Lingering at the door, the little girl immediately notices a number of things. First, Roy Machin and Raymond Wilson, two boys from her council estate, are sitting at a table, laboriously copying the letters on a sheet of paper. Doris and Edith, also from the estate, are sitting opposite them. Her eyes swivel to take in the classroom. At the other tables unknown children are reading. The little girl instantly recognises the very familiar Janet and John reading series. She and her mother had been reading the books since she was three and she had recently started to teach her younger sister to read Book 1. The teacher looks up, smiles and asks her name, then walks over to the desk to check the register. "Sit over there", she says, pointing to a seat between Roy and Doris. The little girl hesitates. She wants to read, and anyway she can write the alphabet on her own. She doesn't need to copy. The little girl's father has told her two things about school: "Be polite and put your hand up when you ask anything", and always speak out if things are unfair. She puts her hand up. The teacher frowns, a twinge of irritation fleeting across her face. "Yes," she enquires. The little girl says very slowly and solemnly "Please Miss, I can read. Can I sit at one of the other tables?" The teacher's frown deepens. "You sit where you are told." The little girl reluctantly slides into her chair but refuses to pick up a pencil, stung by the unfairness of it all. She wrestles with herself and fidgets until the teacher comes across and this time raises her voice. "What on earth is the matter with you, child?" The little girl looks up and says, "But Miss, I can read" – and is made to stand in the corner with her face to the wall for her insolence; but the next day she is moved to a table of readers!

This is a move away from the children I know and am familiar with, to a group whose mothers have told them not to sit with children like me. To remain with my friends means to not progress educationally, while to join those who are seen to be educational achievers is to be positioned as the unwelcome outsider. That was the first time, but far from the last, that I felt a deep sense of relief mingled with fear and an acute sense of disloyalty. Stubborn determination became the hallmark of my schooling. During my primary school years I hovered around 20th out of 46 or so children in my class in the end-of-year tests. My end-of-year report when I was aged eight concluded that 'if Diane continues to work hard she should do quite well'. Faint praise indeed, but then the commonplace understanding was that kids from the estate were stupid.

However, by the end of primary school I was coming second or third in class and had passed the 11-plus, and by the beginning of my second year at grammar school was in the top set. But I was already counting the costs. On my first day at grammar school one of the girls from the private prep school had wafted over with her friends to tell me 'my family knows your family'. When I gave her a puzzled look she retorted, 'your grandmother was our servant', and drifted away. Although she was in a number of top-set classes with me, she never spoke to me again. I learnt from this, and myriad other daily micro acts of class discrimination, to fade into the background, to become as small and invisible as I could make myself. My upper sixth report concludes, 'Diane is a very quiet, thoughtful, intelligent pupil but she rarely speaks and makes very little contribution to class discussions'.

The next extract is from 1970, when I was 20, and is the reference I left university with after obtaining a degree in Politics and Economics. It was written by my personal tutor. I had just received a mark of 70% for my dissertation, which he had supervised.

> I have known Miss Reay for 2 and a half years, nearly one year of which as her tutor, and can vouch for her unimpeachable character and personality. She is a very personable and agreeable girl, always sensible and extremely well presented. She is a conscientious and reliable person with a strong dose of innate intelligence and practical ability. Furthermore, Miss Reay possesses a co-operative and sensible disposition, while her honesty and integrity are beyond question.

Before I went to university I had a part-time job in Woolworths, and this reference, I suggest, is the sort that would have been very helpful in getting me a junior supervisory position in Woolworths. When I read it I felt simultaneously upset and betrayed, but I was also struck by a powerful sense of recognition. I did not challenge it because, on one level, I felt that this man had seen the real as opposed to the fabricated me – the shop girl rather than the aspiring academic. So I gave up on academia, an academic career and trying to be a political researcher, and did not go back for 20 years. This was one of many tumblings-down, of periods spent wrestling with snakes rather than shooting up ladders. Instead, like many of Jackson and Marsden's sample, I became a teacher by default. Over half of Jackson and Marsden's 88 working-class young people – and in the case of the girls, three-quarters – had become teachers, often like me by default or in order to remain in an environment where they could feel a sense of achievement. It was only after I wrote this that I found a very similar analogy in *Education and the Working Class*. One of Jackson and Marsden's successful working-class young men, Mr Beckworth, complained that his struggle to gain a good job was 'like playing at snakes and ladders, only my kind being the kind that comes down the snakes'.

What I am trying to convey through these snapshots of my own and others' social mobility journeys are the 'feelings of being torn that come from experiencing success as failure, or, better still, as transgression'.[8] There is an underlying fragile balance between realising potential and maintaining a sense of authenticity. Almost by definition, working-class aspiration is pretentious, a hankering after 'the other' rather than an acceptance of the self. The powerful yearning that drives social mobility is never fulfilled; rather, it produces an individual caught between two worlds.

The next example, a searing account of class shame and betrayal expressed by the film director Steve McQueen in an interview with Decca Aitkenhead, is from 1980s schooling.[9] When asked to consider how he managed to achieve success from a poor, black, working-class background McQueen was initially hesitant and uncertain:

> I don't know, I'm struggling. I'm struggling here. I've never examined myself. This is hard because I'm going back to certain times in my life I haven't really thought about for a long time. And maybe I avoided that because it was always a very difficult time in a way, and a lot of people were damaged on that journey, friends of mine. And it was all because of people not giving a fuck.

He went on to explain that in his secondary school, by the age of 13, one class of academically gifted kids had been creamed off for special attention. There was 3C1 class: "For, like, OK, normal kids." And then there was 3C2: "For manual labour, more plumbers and builders, stuff like that." McQueen was put in 3C2. At first, he says mildly, "I don't know why. Maybe I deserved to be," and seems about to drop the subject. Moments later:

> That inequality – I fucking loathe it with a passion. It's all bullshit, man. It really upsets me. [...] It was horrible. It was disgusting, the system, it was absolutely disgusting. It's divisive and it was hurtful.

It was awful. School was painful because I just think that loads of people, so many beautiful people, didn't achieve what they could achieve because no one believed in them, or gave them a chance, or invested any time in them. A lot of beautiful boys, talented people, were put by the wayside. School was scary for me because no one cared, and I wasn't good at it because no one cared. At 13 years old, you are marked, you are dead, that's your future.

What these narratives demonstrate is that it is one thing to get out of a social class, but a totally different thing to get into another one that represents the remote and unassailable. McQueen's responses are very different to Bragg's: full of rage and a sense of righteous indignation at how the system, and in particular the education system, works. But both reveal the trauma and negativity that bite into the positive aspects of moving across a huge amount of social space – a rags-to-riches trajectory. In the light of the examples so far it appears as if the socially mobile individual is frequently caught between two worlds, and never fully integrated into either. There is also a potent sense of loss that is rarely recognised under the positive gloss that encompasses the myth of social mobility.

Social mobility in the 21st century: the more things change, the more they stay the same

The analysis so far locates social class as the main factor in understanding social mobility, but social mobility is also always gendered and raced. In my self-funded research in 2015 with young black and minority ethnic BME students in an East London sixth form, groups from different ethnicities had different social mobility trajectories. For many of the African students from Somalia, Eritrea, Nigeria and Uganda, class narratives were about downward mobility through migration to the UK. Parents, and often grandparents, were university educated in their country of origin, although parents were often working in non-graduate jobs in the UK – as taxi drivers, care workers and service sector staff. For these students the central

motif of their narratives was the restoration of the lost status
and economic capital that had accompanied their families'
migration to the UK. The narratives of the Bangladeshi and
Pakistani students were different, although they too spoke of
highly aspirational parents, in particular mothers. Their parents
often felt a keen sense of deprivation in relation to education,
and young people talked about how one or both parents had
been forced to leave school early for the sake of family finances.
Here the central motif of the narratives was one of reparation,
making good past losses and sacrifices.

The case study I am going to focus on is that of Akim, an
18-year-old Bangladeshi student. Both Akim's parents left school
before the age of 16. Akim and his three younger siblings spent
over two years in women's refuges because of his father's violence
towards his mother. He ended up attending five different primary
schools and two secondary schools. His first ambition was to be
a doctor, although there is no one in his family who has been
a doctor. But he did talk about spending time in hospitals as a
young boy because his father regularly beat his mother up.

> Akim: *The teachers thought because of where I come from I was
> thick and my teachers all said I was only fit for Foundation and
> it wasn't until I was in the thick of it I realised how it stopped
> me from realising my dreams, so I got seven Cs and only one A
> star for RE [religious education] because that was the only one I
> wasn't in Foundation for. So it was all a mess and there was no
> way I was going to be a doctor after that. I felt like I will never
> realise my mum's, like my dreams. So I got to 16 and I had
> already failed in life.*
>
> Diane: *So didn't you get any support from the school?*
>
> Akim: *(laughs) I did see a career advisor once. She suggested I do
> vocational work so that wasn't very helpful either.*

In this quote Akim makes a telling slip of the tongue: he first talks
about realising his mother's dreams before correcting himself.
His narrative also reveals a shockingly deficit view of his ability

that translates into self-blame – he has failed himself rather than being failed by his teachers.

Although his experience at the sixth form college has not been as difficult and unsupported as his time in school, it too has been affected by setbacks.

> Akim: *I got two Bs and a C after a year of AS so started again three totally different subjects and then I got two As and a B so it was worth it cos now I am predicted three As.*

Akim also illustrates a total ignorance about what is involved in going to university, accompanied by a lot of anxiety at the prospect. Akim has received five offers ranging from three As to one A and two Bs, but still talks about being worried about whether he will get in.

> Akim: *I am really scared about going to uni, I know I have to go because there is no other choice but I don't know how I'll cope. I have no idea what I am letting myself in for.*

> Diane: *So why are you going?*

> Akim: *I want to do it because I really want to help my mum and my brothers, there is no one else to help them.*

> Diane: *But what about you, what do you want to do for you, because you are sounding like you don't actually want to be a lawyer?*

> Akim: *(laughs) Not really, but my mum was always having to see lawyers and they weren't a lot of good so I am going to be one of the good guys.*

This does not sound like an individualised project of self-advancement but much more of a family project grounded in the hardships and adversity experienced not only by himself but also by his mother and siblings. Akim, like many of the other young people I interviewed, is concerned to change the world along with his own personal circumstances. But commitments and attachments are not equal to changing the world.

Social mobility comes with a neoliberal vocabulary of aspiration, ambition, choice and self-efficacy, but I suggest that there are strong elements of compulsion in Akim's narrative. He has no choice but to try to put things right. Also, there is no sense of confidence or entitlement about the enterprise but, rather, a frightening cocktail of fear, bewilderment and ignorance. There are powerful resonances here with Jackson and Marsden's finding in the 1960s that higher education was approached by the young people they interviewed with a mixture of sheer ignorance and general perplexity. His lack of knowledge also mirrored my own 50 years earlier. I had decided I wanted to go to the London School of Economics (LSE) because I had heard it was the best training ground for political researchers, as well as having a left-wing, radical reputation. My head teacher and deputy head had other ideas. They summoned me to a meeting in which they told me "girls like you do not go to LSE". When I demurred, I was told it was a place for aristocrats and the rich upper classes, people I would not fit in with. So my mum and I sat down and wrote a letter to the advice page of the *Daily Mirror* asking for a list of working-class universities. The reply mentioned only two – Sheffield and Newcastle. Neither was working class, although they could be considered to be in working-class cities. I had relatives in Newcastle, so I went there. Like Akim's, my decision was rooted in ignorance, compounded by misinformation and a sense of having no choice. I ended up 'making do'. Akim too talked about "having to make do" and "put up with [his] current situation". He told me "it is just the way it has to be". But a relentless focus on a better future suspends questions about the cruelty of the present.

When I asked Akim what influenced young people's opportunities in England today he said money and background, and then made a joke about having no money and having no useful connections. He spoke about how he had really known next to nothing about how education worked, and that by the time he found out he had already made the wrong choices and it was too late to do what he really wanted to do. In an e-mail

Akim sent me in January 2016 from his Russell Group university, he wrote:

> It has been a really scary and stressful first term. I didn't really have a clue what to expect, everything has been tougher than I was expecting, and I still haven't settled in. It doesn't help that there is no one like me here.

Although it is not for me to speculate, choosing to do law in an already overcrowded graduate law market may well turn out to be another problematic choice for Akim. Both medicine and law are popular choices for young Asian students, but not for young, working-class Bangladeshi boys with no professionals in either their families or social networks. Rather, I want to suggest that Akim's choices lay in his mother's painful experiences in hospitals and lawyers' offices, that a strong motivation lay in desiring to 'put things right', to repair what had gone wrong. He has also assumed this massive undertaking without access to any economic, social and cultural capital. The almost intolerable psychic burden this placed on him was evident throughout the interview, but was most poignantly revealed at the end of the interview when he began to weep, before apologising and commenting that it had been a relief to get it all off his chest because there wasn't really anyone to talk to, especially as he didn't want to worry his mum. And Akim is not a unique case: five other BME young people at the sixth form spoke of parents who had serious illnesses – multiple sclerosis, schizophrenia, chronic arthritis and serious depression; four wanted to go on to study medical sciences, to become doctors, physiotherapists, and psychologists, and all their accounts, at times, seemed to be more about a project of retrospective healing rather than an individualised project of upward mobility. Their struggle for a good life was not only for themselves but for their families, communities and society more widely. Underlying their social mobility projects are very different sentiments from the self-seeking motives usually attributed to the socially mobile.

Young people like Akim are attempting to put right something that is not their responsibility; they are trying to correct wider historic social ills and injuries that they have not personally caused. But in deeply unequal societies like England today, redressing gross unfairness is no longer seen to be the responsibility of the powerful in society, so it is left to young people like Akim to repair the historic and continuing damage inflicted on their families. In 21st-century England social, political and economic inequalities have been transformed into educational inequalities that then become the responsibility of the individual.

Commonalities and differences in mobility stories

There has been a gender imbalance in this chapter so far; these have been predominantly men's tales, and reflect the history of social mobility over the last century as tales of working-class men made good. I want to underscore some of these themes of oscillation, ambivalence, guilt and inauthenticity that have emerged in the above examples of social mobility by looking at the work of Valerie Walkerdine, Helen Lucey and Steph Lawler. Walkerdine and Lucey argue that upward mobility was something that all of the working-class women in their study met with deep ambivalence.[10] Retaining emotional and material links with parents was key to psychic survival, and yet it was also often felt as a burden which the women could not escape from. These themes are echoed in Steph Lawler's work on narratives of women's upward mobility in which 'the fantasy of "getting out and getting away" may be achieved only at the price of entering another set of social relations, in which the assumed pathology of their (working-class women's) history and their desires is brought home to them more intensely'.[11] This feminist work stresses the need to understand upward mobility as having a deeply defensive aspect. The discourses through which to read upward mobility present it as a freeing, a success. But striving for success for a working-class young person is about wanting something different, something more than your parents had, and that not only implies that there is something wrong with your parents' life, but that there is something intrinsically wrong with them. And there is an emptiness to becoming somebody if your parents remain nobodies. What is the point of striving for equality with more-privileged others if the process creates inequalities between you and the people you love, and the communities you were born into? I want to argue that a tension between success for the individual at the expense of the failure of the many is a key motif in the narratives of many of the socially mobile. Berlant writes of shame as 'the darker side of aspiration's optimism'.[12] And there is shame in both belonging and escape – shame in escape because it is about betrayal and desertion, but also shame in belonging because, in a strongly classed society like the UK, despite conflicting feelings of political connection and pride, a sense of belonging to the working classes carries connotations of being less.

But I also want to argue, as you can see both in the example of Akim and in my own experience, that longing for something different and then striving to make this happen constitutes an emotionally and socially terrifying shift away from the safe and familiar that is pervaded with setbacks and fallings-down. Social mobility is often presented as a straightforward linear process from one occupational category to another, but when we look at the lived experience of social mobility it is full of doublings-back, loops and curves, culs-de-sac and diversions.

What we also learn from both Jackson and Marsden's research and the experiences of Akim and the other BME students in my study is that sometimes this longing for something different is a family project: the longing is invested in parents, and particularly the mother, as much as in the child. And sometimes this longing is not for something entirely different but is part of a family project of restoration, of reinstating the family to what is seen to be its rightful social position; and always the amount of social space to be traversed is key. As a 2016 research study of Australian 'rags to riches' trajectories found, these are often 'meandering journeys that entail great humility, a desire to maintain pride in one's roots, and for many, an intention to keep travelling back to family and communities of origin, for love and professional service'.[13] But, as the examples I have drawn on indicate, this is easier said than done. Rags-to-riches trajectories are always the most celebrated and glamorised, but they carry the risks of alienation and dislocation, of never finding a place to belong. It is much easier to traverse a small amount of social space than to leap from the top to the bottom. This is why Jackson and

Marsden write so poignantly of the nine boys who went to Oxbridge as lost souls. In their case study of Henry Dibb they describe how he won an open scholarship to Cambridge, taking a first in his exams after the first year. But later he questioned his education, and specifically the social side of it. He lamented that his tutor "more or less gave up on me", and he ended up with a third-class degree. He returned to his home town and took up manual work, but found it unrewarding and soul destroying. As Jackson and Marsden point out, 'he couldn't be working class and he didn't want to be middle class'.[14]

The key point is that people like myself, Akim, Steve McQueen and Walkerdine and Lucey's young women want to rise with their class, not out of it. Yet the optimism, hopes and desires that come with social mobility are doomed to disappointment because raising the class has to be a collective social endeavour. Social mobility, or rather its failure, is presented as if it is a personal trouble that resides within the 'character of the individual' and depends upon the effort and agency of the individual. Yet, as C. Wright Mills argued in 1943, working-class social mobility needs to be seen as a public issue that transcends the individual.[15] The nature of social mobility in English society is a consequence of the way society is historically organised 'as a whole'. Social mobility, particularly in deeply unequal societies, is always about failure as much as it is about success. You become more equal in relation to privileged others, but at the cost of those you love and care for becoming less equal in relation to you.

The cruel optimism that generates and sustains social mobility journeys is, as Moore and Claire so vividly describe, 'the ultimately self-defeating pursuit of what is hoped for, or desired'.[16] Despite feelings of relief, good fortune and gratitude, social mobility narratives that describe 'a rags to riches trajectory' are inevitably stories of dissatisfaction, guilt, internal strife and unrealised dreams and desires. Cruel optimism often leads to a nagging sense of mutation rather than wholeness, Bragg's 'class mongrel', Jackson and Marsden's 'lost souls' and Lawler's guilty escapees.

Outsiders on the inside: the working classes and higher education

I feel an idiot. I guess I just didn't get the right advice so I started my law degree thinking that was all I needed to be a human rights lawyer and of course it's nowhere near enough. So now I am doing a Master's and my debt level is over £50,000 ... and I'm suddenly thinking how on earth am I going to get a job as a lawyer. I'll probably still be working in Next in five years' time and the only difference between me and the other shop assistants is that I've got shed-loads of debt.

Lisa, a working-class full-time Master's student at a red-brick university, and whose mother is herself a shop assistant, is working 15 hours a week in Next as well as doing 12 hours of bar work, just to keep her head above the water financially. In her interview with me she talked of feeling trapped in education, that it felt far too risky to leave with just an undergraduate degree but terrifying to go on acquiring debts that she could not foresee ever paying off. Lisa is one of the growing number of educationally successful working-class students, 'outsiders on the inside', caught up in an educational conveyor belt that all too often leads to disappointment and debts rather than the realisation of their dreams.

The increasingly unequal higher education landscape: the elitist underpinning of mass higher education

One area of education where politicians claim there is notable success is in relation to widening access and participation in higher education. In much of the political rhetoric the success of social mobility is judged in terms of getting more and more working-class young people to go to university. And yes, over the two decades since 1997 more and more working-class students have gone on to higher education (although this has recently been reversed for white, working-class males).[17] However, while the increasing numbers are lauded in the press and policy announcements, what is neglected is the debt these working-class students accrue in the process, and the types of universities they are going to. In 21st-century Britain class inequalities in higher education have shifted from being primarily about exclusion from the system to being about exclusion within it. In the UK, children from working-class backgrounds account for just 1 in 20 enrolments into the elite Russell Group of universities.[18] When we focus on the poorest category within the British working class (those on FSM), the percentage who go on to attend elite universities, including Oxbridge, drops to 0.9%.[19] Private school students are 55 times more likely than FSM students to gain a place at Oxford or Cambridge. These are enormous disparities in access that are only partly explained by the poorer entry qualifications of applicants from working-class backgrounds.

Just as concerning is the large gap between working-class applications and admissions, as disparities in rates of admission to the elite universities remain substantial for working-class applicants, even after entry qualifications have been taken into account.[20] Research in 2013 showed that middle-class students are three times more likely to go to elite universities than are working-class pupils, even if they have the same grades,[21] and that institutional stratification within English higher education strengthened between 1996 and 2010, especially at the top end of the hierarchy and towards the end of the period.[22] Adding to this gloomy picture, research looking at graduates who obtained their degrees between 1996 and 2009 shows that there was an increase of slightly under 10% among those from middle-class backgrounds,[23] but of just 5% among those from working-class backgrounds.[24] More recent research from the Higher Education Statistics Agency (HESA) shows that the percentage of students from poor backgrounds going to Cambridge fell from 12.4% to 10.2% between 2005 and 2016.[25] In addition, there is concern about retaining working-class students and ensuring their progress. In the UK, those universities with the most success at widening participation to working-class students are predominantly those that are perceived to be low status. They are also the universities with the highest drop-out rates. Approximately one in five undergraduate students leaves university without gaining a degree, and research has shown that working-class students attending lower-status universities are disproportionately likely to drop out.[26]

So, working-class students are increasingly going to university, and accumulating debts of at least £30,000 and often much more, without accruing anything like the returns of their upper- and middle-class peers. As research in 2016 concludes, working-class young people who do go to university are less likely to graduate and less likely to achieve the highest degree classes.[27] And, it is the least well-off of the working-class students who have to borrow the most, since maintenance grants for the poorest students were replaced by loans in 2016. Whereas in the past students from families with a household income of £25,000 or less were entitled to a grant of £3,387 per year to cover living costs, they now have to take out a loan.[28] As Peter Lampl, chairman of the Sutton Trust, argued:

> The abolition of maintenance grants means it is the poorest graduates who are getting the worst deal, with debts of over £50,000 on graduation. It is outrageous that the government has got rid of maintenance grants. It will make it harder to increase the numbers of disadvantaged students at the most selective universities and it will lumber them with massive debts. With the access gap at these universities still unacceptably wide, the government should be doing all it can to increase participation, not reduce it.

A question of who goes where and how they feel about it

Working-class students are predominantly going to universities that are seen to be low status and 'second rate'. The growing stratification of the higher education field is increasingly apparent in the very differing levels of resources across the university sector, but it is also there in students' common-sense understandings of 'good' and 'poor' universities. Together with Gill Crozier and John Clayton, I conducted a study of working-class students in four universities spread across the universities league table. How the higher education institution that these working-class students attended was classified exerted a powerful influence on how they saw themselves and were seen by others in terms of both their learner and class identities.[29] The following is just one of many quotes that divided universities into good and bad. Kylie is talking about how other students on her MA course will react when they hear that she has done her first degree at Northern, a university near the bottom of the league table.

> *I'm going to be sitting there on the first day scared to open my mouth because as soon as I say something, they'll be like "who the hell's that? Is she one of the locals?" Do you know what I mean? I can just tell how they're going to look at uz. Especially when I say I went to [Northern], that's just going to be even worse, and they're all going to have gone to really good universities, aren't they? It'll be like you went to the polytechnic at [Northern] (laughs), that's what they'll be saying.*

Some of the students, from working-class as well as middle-class backgrounds, talked of Northern as 'a rubbish university'. Northern's reputation suffered from it being categorised as 'a working-class' university, with all the reputational losses that came from such a label.

As I have argued earlier, the working-class relationship to schooling has typically been one of failure,[30] and this was still true for how a majority of the Northern students perceived their university experience. As Arthur, a white, working-class history student at Northern, said:

> *My thoughts have always been, at my lowest point, it's always that I'm not capable of doing it.*

And as Barbara, another white, working-class history student at Northern, suggested:

> *Academically wise I keep thinking I shouldn't be here, that you know I'm not up to the level that I should be.*

Both Arthur and Barbara are mature students with, as Arthur points out, a considerable gap between school and university, but even the young students lacked confidence in their own academic ability.

Unfortunately, my experiences of school always taught me that, I mean I was always a late learner, I never caught on particularly quickly but when I did it was always slightly later. So I was always brought up with the attitude that "oh, Katy will never amount to anything". (Katy, white, working-class chemistry student, Northern)

A majority of working-class students end up in universities seen to be 'second class' by both themselves and others. And, as Bourdieu and Champagne assert, 'after an extended school career, which often entails considerable sacrifice, the most culturally disadvantaged run the risk of ending up with a devalued degree'.[31] Even now, when increasing numbers of working-class students have access to higher education, class inequalities reappear in the unequal access to forms of valued cultural and social capital, as the middle classes monopolise both those universities seen to be the 'best' and high-status, esteemed activities and social networks within the less prestigious universities.[32] The success of the few working-class students who do gain entry to UK elite universities has a negligible impact on this broader picture of continuing classed and racialised inequalities.

In the same study, a major factor impacting on working-class university experience, and the students' chances of integrating fully into the field of higher education, was the university they attended.[33] What we also found in our research was that the rewards and recognition of going to university were nearly always lower for the working-class students than for their middle- and upper-class peers. Of course, we want more ethnic minority and working-class students to go to university, but when they primarily go to poor, 'working-class' universities in a segregated system, we are talking about a very unlevel playing field. So it is much more than an issue of widening access. The troubling paradox of widening access and the democratisation of higher education is that, despite the democratic intentions, widening access has brought an intensification of class and racial inequalities between different levels of higher education. Growing diversity within the field of higher education, rather than producing a more inclusive higher education, has resulted in a segregated and increasingly polarised system. Upper- and upper middle-class pursuit of the educational exclusivity experienced in private and selective state schooling has relegated the working classes and the lower middle classes to the universities that the more privileged do not want to attend. This signals a growing exclusivity at the top of the higher education hierarchy.

The myth of meritocracy in the 21st century

In order to fully understand the way class works as a form of educational exclusion within higher education we need to step back and examine not only the mission and purpose of elite universities like Oxbridge but also how they justify and explain their selectivity and elitism to themselves and others. This requires an interrogation of the meritocratic ideal that Oxbridge and other elite universities hold dear. It also requires an analysis of the powerful ways in which educational systems, including their universities, work to reproduce the existing order rather than to transform it.

When Michael Young coined the term 'meritocracy' in his 1958 satire *The Rise of the Meritocracy*, he introduced into popular understanding an ideal long cherished in British society: 'may the best person win'.[34] The meritocratic paradigm, if not the term itself, has been a cornerstone of liberal and social democratic thought for the last two centuries. And despite Young's pessimistic account of the dangers of meritocracy, it has become widely accepted as an ideal in liberal democratic societies. A meritocratic system is a competition in which there are clear winners and losers, but in which the resulting inequalities are justified on the basis that participants have an equal opportunity to prove themselves. The fantasy made clear in *The Rise of Meritocracy* is that the 'best' educational system is a meritocratic one. But in the 21st century the reality is that it has become a powerful means of legitimising both social exclusion and elitism.[35] We have an educational system where the norm is to misrecognise and reward the benefits of a privileged class background as deriving from individual effort and ability.[36] As Alan Fox wrote a number of years before Young's 'Myth of the Meritocracy' was published, meritocracy is:

the society in which the gifted, the smart, the energetic, the ambitious and the ruthless are carefully sifted out and helped towards their destined positions of dominance, where they proceed not only to enjoy the fulfilment of exercising their natural endowments but also to receive a fat bonus thrown in for good measure.[37]

I would add the 'rich' to the list above, although it is probably implicit in Fox's words. A crucial part of the operation of reproducing the British elite and nurturing and expanding its academic, cultural and social capital is carried out by Oxbridge and a small number of other elite universities.[38] As a consequence, Oxbridge remains the equivalent of 'a finishing school' for the private school system, polishing, refining and accentuating the elitism and sense of superiority acquired in earlier schooling. What is clear is that clinging to the meritocratic principle as a way of achieving fairness in relation to university admission and participation will not work. Since the early 1990s sociologists of education have been pointing out that educational choice is based on the resources and social power and networks of the parents rather than the ability and effort of the child.[39] Meritocracy has become the educational equivalent of the emperor with no clothes, all ideological bluff with no substance. We do not have a meritocracy, or anything approaching a meritocracy. Yet, the elite universities continue to justify their elitism on the premise that they operate in a meritocratic society.

A higher education system that rewards the richest

As Tables 5.1 and 5.2 indicate, the issue of resources and funding raises uncomfortable and difficult issues around value in which views of moral and intellectual value are entangled with, and expressed through, levels of monetary value. The new opportunities for the working-class have diminished value because they are studying in low-ranking universities with 'too many' students like themselves who are perceived to be 'low status'. As Table 5.2 makes evident, in the neoliberal market economy of higher education the low value attributed to the working-class translates into poorly funded courses in inadequately resourced universities, while the rich are seen to merit generously funded courses in wealthy universities.

Table 5.1: Top 10 universities, by income per full-time equivalent student, 2010/11 (£k)

Cambridge	65.84
Imperial College	48.82
Oxford	46.82
University College London	37.61
Edinburgh	27.77
London School of Economics	26.24
King's College London	25.87
Bristol	23.74
Liverpool	23.47
Warwick	22.17

Source: Brown, 2012.

Table 5.2: Bottom 10 universities, by income per full-time equivalent student, 2010/11 (£k)

Chester	8.04
Bath Spa	7.97
Leeds Metropolitan	7.93
West of Scotland	7.91
Abertay Dundee	7.80
Swansea Met	7.57
Wales Newport	7.57
Wales Trinity St David	7.20
Glamorgan	7.08
Edge Hill	7.05

Source: Brown, 2012.

But it is not just the stark differences in resources and funding within higher education that make the working-class experience of higher education very different to that of many middle- and upper-class students. As Stevenson and Clegg found in their 2011 research, due to forces of circumstance, the majority of the working-class students were trapped in the present as 'onlookers' on student life, compelled by economic necessity to live at home and work in the labour market.[40] In our study, working-class students were far more likely to be exhausted from part-time work, distracted by financial, health and family problems, and often lacking the confidence and self-esteem to be able to construct themselves as successful learners.[41] They were jostling competing demands that undermined their ability to adapt and integrate into higher education. Widening access to a very unequal, hierarchical field is a very crude response to an intractable problem that requires a much more sophisticated, morally informed solution. And just how rich many Oxbridge students are is graphically revealed in the research results from a 2009 student survey published in *Varsity*, the Cambridge student newspaper (Table 5.3)

Although these income levels are now almost 10 years out of date, they represent salary levels that most English families can only dream of. Cambridge and Oxford are primarily universities for the rich in a country where 90% of the population earn less than £50,000 a year and 75% earn less than £30,000.[42]

Table 5.3: Average annual parental income for Cambridge colleges, 2009

College	Average annual parental income
Murray Edwards	£108,000
Caius	£96,100
Clare	£85,100
Trinity	£82,800
Emmanuel	£82,400
Pembroke	£80,600
Robinson	£79,200
Corpus	£78,500
Downing	£77,900
Selwyn	£77,900
Magdalene	£75,800
King's	£75,500
Churchill	£72,500
Christ's	£70,900
Girton	£69,900
Trinity Hall	£69,800
Queen's	£68,800
Jesus	£68,000
Sidney Sussex	£67,100
Newnham	£66,800
Fitzwilliam	£64,500
St John's	£63,900
St Catharine's	£58,500
Homerton	£55,100
Peterhouse	£54,800

Source: Varsity (2009)

Conclusion

In this chapter I have tried to demonstrate the many ways in which social mobility in a deeply unequal society like England's is not the panacea it is made out to be. And the focus on meritocracy is a smoke screen diverting attention from the ways in which the educational system positions the vast majority of the working-class as devalued 'outsiders within'. As Jo Littler points out, currently, in both the UK and the US, the focus on meritocracy is being used to justify policies that will increase rather than decrease inequality.[43] The key issue we need to tackle in education is not social mobility but inequality. Far from being a solution, social mobility creates social and educational problems even as it provides a degree of success for a small number of working-class individuals.

The huge expansion of higher education in England is often presented as evidence of the success of social mobility and meritocracy in English society. But, just as in relation to the school system, the inequalities permeating higher education are damaging for all university students. The 'winner takes all' ethos, and the intense competition and striving for academic excellence that underpin it, have taken their toll across social classes. In 2013 a survey by student newspaper *The Tab* revealed that 21% of Cambridge students have been diagnosed with depression, while a further 25% think they may be depressed. The problem disproportionately affects female students. In all-female college Murray Edwards, 28% of students have experienced eating disorders. The numbers are reflected more widely: the National Union of Students surveyed 1,200 students and found that 20% believe they have a mental health problem, while 1 in 10 had experienced suicidal thoughts.[44] Welfare teams at Cambridge alone anticipate 50 to 60 suicide attempts per year. As Wilkinson and Pickett demonstrated so powerfully in 2009, inequality, in a culture of hyper-competitive individualism, reduces everyone's sense of well-being.[45]

But, as I have highlighted in relation to the school sector, while all students are affected by the inequalities of the university sector, it is working-class students who suffer the most, and the unfairness they face continues even after they have left university.

Working-class students will now graduate with an average of £14,000 more debt than their wealthier peers.[46] Graduates from the poorest 40 per cent of families have average debts of £57,000 compared with £43,000 for the richest 30 per cent.[47] They are also to be found disproportionately in unsalaried or low-paid posts six months after leaving university.[48] Overall, 58.8% of graduates are in jobs deemed to be non-graduate roles, according to a report by the Chartered Institute of Personnel and Development, a percentage exceeded only in Greece and Estonia,[49] and it is working-class graduates in the new universities who are likely to end up getting working-class jobs. But working-class students at elite universities are also seriously disadvantaged as compared to their middle-class peers. Coulson et al found that, of the working-class students on a special-entry scheme to an elite Russell Group university, 57% gained graduate jobs, as compared to 74% of graduates university-wide. This was despite a higher percentage of these working-class students gaining a first or upper second degree than the general student population.[50]

Even when working-class students do attain graduate jobs they will find that the much-vaunted graduate premium is much less than they were promised. Britton et al's research shows that students from higher-income families have median earnings that are around 25% more than those of students from lower-income families.[51] As Crawford et al found, class differences in graduate earnings persisted even when educational attainment, including university attended and subject studied, is taken into account.[52] Recent research discovered that people from working-class backgrounds who get a professional job receive salaries on average £6,800 (17%) less than those of their middle- and upper-class colleagues.[53] They identify the 'stickiness' of class origin, in which a poverty of resources in early life often continues to shape individual life courses well beyond occupational entry.

If you are working class, even a high-class degree from a top university does not provide equality of access to top professions and higher earnings. The sad irony is that as more and more working-class students have achieved a degree, its status has been eroded and the value in which it is held, both symbolically and in financial terms, has dropped.[54] The DfE Longitudinal Education

Outcomes survey found that as student numbers have increased, graduate earning power has decreased in relation to non-graduate earnings. As the survey concludes, future continuing increases in numbers of graduates would result in further declines in the educational wage differential.[55]

The fallacy that sending more and more working-class young people to university constitutes social mobility has become a common belief. Yet, producing more and more working-class graduates in a restricted labour market for graduates is a perverse form of social mobility. The consequences can be seen in the working-class female PhD graduate who has been serving in my local restaurant for three years, and the male Master's graduate who has been working at the check-out in the local supermarket for nearly five years. Can either Rosie or Assiz be called socially mobile when both are in casualised and poorly paid work? Although highly credentialled, both are desperate and despairing about their lack of economic progression. As I have argued earlier in the chapter, these are the educationally successful working-class who no longer see themselves as working class but are striving to become middle class. They have a fragile relationship to the working-class communities they have come from, but also to the middle-class society they are struggling to belong to.

To conclude, in contrast to the rose-tinted view of social mobility in both political and popular understandings, at the collective level it constitutes a form of asset stripping of the working-classes, while at the individual level it often results in ambivalence, dislocation and a sense of belonging to neither the class one has come from nor the class one has nominally joined. As one working-class student at Cambridge told me:

> You know you are privileged, you know you have done extremely, well but you have nowhere you really belong to and that can feel very lonely.

SIX

The middle and upper classes: getting the 'best' for your own child

Introduction

Social class is a relational concept in which working-class experiences do not make sense unless they are contextualised within the wider class hierarchy. We cannot understand working-class experiences of education without looking at how both the upper and middle classes are positioned within education, their educational practices and how these in turn impact on working-class students. This chapter is divided into three sections. The first looks at the 'elite' middle and upper classes who send their children to private school, while the second section examines the middle classes who send their children to predominantly working-class, urban schools; in both cases, the upper- and middle-class understandings of their relationships with their 'class' others are foregrounded. In the last section I return to the consequences for the working classes of middle- and upper-class attitudes and actions at university level. A specific focus within the chapter is the status of the middle classes as 'the ideal normative class' within state education, and the consequences for the working classes. The conclusion argues that although the upper and middle classes benefit from an educational system that historically has been set up to serve their interests, they are also, to an extent, damaged by the invidious workings of an inequitable system that emphasises divisions and hierarchy at the expense of commonalities and what different groups in society share.

The narratives of the privileged class groups reveal both potent defences and a sense of superiority, but also the power of emotions. All these elements are explored through a number of case studies that highlight complex moral and ethical dimensions of upper- and middle-class identity and, in particular, emotional responses to the class 'other' that both feed into and arise from 'principled' and 'not so principled' choices. Upper- and middle-class relationships to those in other class and racial groups are central to their class identities, and the chapter examines the powerful affective work that both relationships and representations do in the formation of upper- and middle-class identities.

The upper classes and the certainties of privilege

In this section I draw on data to show the implicit, taken-for-granted elements of elite middle- and upper-class choice. In a research project on higher education choice 28 students who attended two elite private schools and 15 of their parents were interviewed.[1] What was striking after interviewing many working-class parents was the certainty and confidence with which these privileged parents approached their children's schooling. There were neither the hyper-anxiety of many middle-class parents sending their children to state schools nor the doubts and lack of confidence of working-class parents. In their place was an almost unassailable belief that their children were, and would continue to be, educational successes. I was told that their children were 'incredibly bright', 'destined for academic heights', 'bound for Oxbridge' and 'simply brilliant at sciences'. Bourdieu writes that those who move in their world like fish in water do not need to 'engage in rational computation in order to reach the goals that best suit their interests', and these parents and their children demonstrated a self-assured relationship to education.[2] This self-assuredness was evident in their choice of university. They did not even bother to articulate the divide between old and new universities because going to a new university is just not what someone like them does. Where there was sometimes active decision making was in relation to which Oxbridge college to select, or if A Level predicted grades were not all As and A*s, which other Russell Group universities might be acceptable choices. In the extract below Samantha's mother is clear that medicine and Cambridge are already foregone conclusions for Samantha, but she does elaborate on the careful consideration given to which Cambridge college would best suit her daughter.

Ever since Samantha was old enough to know what a doctor was that is all she has ever wanted to do. She never really needed advice. I mean, yes, she went along to various careers lectures and spoke to teachers, whatever, but she never really was that interested. She always knew what she wanted to do.

Dealing with university was probably a very unscientific process actually. My father went to Trinity in Cambridge to do law. And he was always very keen to show her Cambridge and his old college, which he did, when she was probably only about 13. And she fell in love with it. And decided that's where she wanted to go. As time progressed and she learnt about step papers and all the other things that you have to do, she decided Trinity was a bit formidable in terms of getting in, because she hasn't got the hugest amount of confidence, and she thought she'd maybe look for a college that wasn't so difficult, although frankly I think they are all much of a muchness. So she started to look at others, but again, not very scientifically.

She went up on an open day with her careers teacher. And they went for an open day at Clare, I think it was, and while she was there she had a bit of a look around some of the other colleges including Trinity Hall, but just a quick look. A friend of mine had a daughter who had just taken up a place at Trinity Hall to do natural sciences and this friend of mine is very very good at research, all this sort of stuff, and she'd been into huge huge detail and she basically gave me all the benefit of her research and said Trinity Hall is a much smaller college and they may not require step papers, and her daughter had certainly benefited from a smaller college and thought Samantha might as well, and why didn't we look at Trinity Hall? Which is why we looked at Trinity Hall.

And she spoke to her teachers about it and they agreed she should try for Trinity Hall. I don't think anyone else was trying, so that probably helped, and that's how she ended up at Trinity Hall. (Mother of Samantha, a white, upper middle-class, private school student)

Samantha may have to think through which Cambridge college to apply to, but every other part of her life trajectory is determined, predestined from an earlier age. As with the other upper and upper middle-class young people I interviewed, her life was full of certainties. In many respects little seems to have changed for this privileged upper middle-class fraction since Michael Apted made a documentary series for Granada TV called *Seven-Up* that has been tracking the same group of children since 1964. In the series two prep school boys, Andrew and John, end up going to Oxbridge, just as they predicted when they were seven, and become a solicitor and a barrister, respectively. In fact, this section of the middle classes don't have to engage in 'getting the best' for their children, rather it is automatic, taken for granted, simply what happens to 'people like us'. Educational success comes easily to this class group: they have the money, confidence, social connections and resources to make it happen without a great deal of effort.

A sense of intrinsic superiority was explicit in the words of many of the privately educated students whom I interviewed.

I just expected to go to a good university. I knew I was a lot more intelligent and cultured than ordinary kids. (Will, private school student)

An investigation by *Varsity*, the Cambridge student newspaper, found that 40% of students at Cambridge had a family member who had been to Oxbridge.[3] There is a great deal of 'becoming like my mother or father' for the upper and upper middle classes.

There was also a great deal of disparagement and contempt for the class 'other'. In the next extract, from a Cambridge university focus group of privately educated students, we can discern powerful class disdain and a sense of intellectual and moral superiority, and glimpse some of the challenges that working-class students may experience when studying alongside privileged students like Dominic and Marcus:

Dominic: *We occasionally have trouble from the locals, they are all a bit chavvy.*

Diane: *What sort of trouble?*

Dominic: *Well, there was this chav sort of hanging around the quad where the first-years live, um, and he was just hanging around there a lot. I mean, there are some bike parks at the front so I guess he was thinking of stealing a bike or possibly trying to mug some people, it's not well lit. And some students go outside to tell him to get lost and this guy starts causing trouble with the students and the porter, an ex-SAS, goes and beats the living daylights out of him!*

Everyone: *(laughs)*

Marcus: *I shouldn't be saying this! (laugh) but yeah! all the local chavs are just 'scared to death' of him!*

An article in *Varsity* (27 November 2016) included an interview with one of the waitresses serving in a college dining hall, herself a student at another university. The writer reports that the waitress and other dining staff experienced a great deal of coldness, and surmises that it is because the Cambridge ethos encourages in its students 'a self-perception of one's own superiority or one's exceptionality'. Another article (3 June 2015) expressed concern about the derogatory language students use to talk about working-class people – terms like chavs, povos and peasants. But when we look at more informal media like student chatrooms, disdain and condescension can rapidly collapse into class hatred. In a post in 2016 on The Studentroom a Cambridge student commented:

Chavs are the underclass of Britain, the sub-culture of the jobless, ambitionless, nothings, these are the people who are embodying what used to be the respectable working class. They don't deserve our respect, they all need a kick up the arse, and a raid by the counterfeit department in the police. And that's me being nice!

To which another Cambridge student responded:

Indeed at one time the working classes used to break their backs for us. Now what are they good for? I say shoot the buggers.

Other posts from private school students refer to the working classes as 'subhuman', 'toothless', 'uneducated', 'undisciplined', 'morons' and 'thuggish'.

In earlier work I have argued that the economic crisis resulting from the recession and subsequent austerity could result in one of two trends: either reaction and an intensification of protection and safeguarding of class privileges and status, or a more creative and open questioning of the status quo.[4] With hindsight, it has led to neither because the class privilege of parents sending their children to private schools has remained intact without them having to change their practices or, indeed, their attitudes. In fact this is the one group to have emerged with increased wealth and resources. However, the parents and children I discuss next are a complicated and, at times, contradictory mixture of the two trends.

The middle classes and ambivalences of proximity with class 'others'

When we focus on the middle classes who do send their children to state schools we find privileged middle-class enclaves; admittedly not as privileged as many of the private schools, but white, middle-class bubbles nonetheless. Despite a powerful rhetoric of equal opportunities and a flirtation with more inclusive democratic ideals, what the middle classes have always been extremely good at is drawing boundaries and metaphorically pulling up the educational drawbridge in the face of those whom they view as educationally beneath them. Jackson and Marsden, writing about the few working-class children who did make it to grammar school in the 1960s, argue that they were left with a sense of not belonging, isolation and having to accommodate to middle-class values. Our expectation would be that things have changed greatly in the comprehensive system of the 21st century. Yet Kate, one of the middle-class young people in our study on the middle classes sending their children to urban comprehensives, describes how:

> At first my friends and I were really scared about all the chavs there might be at secondary school, that they'd get in the way of our learning. But it turned out fine because after the first year we were all in the top set and they were all in the bottom set, and now they have all left.[5]

In the study Kate was part of, interviews were conducted with 180 parents and 70 children from 125 white, middle-class households in three UK cities. The target group were middle-class parents committed to comprehensive schooling as an educational principle who deliberately avoided 'working the system to their advantage'. In the interviews these parents often identified themselves in opposition to those who sent their children to private school. Only a minority had the confidence and certainty surrounding their choice that the private school parents articulated. They were, in their own words, often inconsistent in terms of their motives, torn in terms of their principles and attempting to manage competing value systems. It is perhaps unsurprising, then, that, despite professed commitments to egalitarianism and communitarian ideals, a significant number of the parents talked about the specialness of their children being boosted in the setting of the ordinary comprehensive. Trudy, for example, was explicit about how her children's 'specialness' could be advantageously enhanced at an 'ordinary' comprehensive school:

> and the other thing which was important to us was, well it was certainly important to me, I don't know if it was important to [my husband], but I wanted my children to stand out, and there are lots of children like [my first] and [second] and [third child] at Wheelers and Waterford and Hammerton [all high-performing schools] actually, and much fewer of them at Redwood – although

it's changing I have to say – and I think that for the girls in particular, that has been a very good experience for them because they're generally in their own personalities, both reasonably … I mean they're clever aren't they? And they're lovely, they're very well behaved, they're responsible, they have been loved for the fact that they're great kids to have in class and they've really benefited from that, their teachers want them in their classes and they've benefited from really good attention because of that…. Well yes, they've made an impact by being nice and by people appreciating them having them in their class.

Interviewer: *So when you say 'I wanted them to stand out.' That's from the teacher's point of view?*

Mother: *Yes. I wanted them to be known, I didn't want them to be anonymous.* (Trudy, white, middle class mother)

But, as both working-class young people and working-class adults regularly pointed out, they often felt overlooked and disregarded in schooling, part of an anonymous backdrop that middle-class children can shine against. Attention, when they did receive it, was often for the wrong reasons, reprimands rather than praise. Here again the importance of class as relational is key. In these middle-class parents' individualised outlook, it is evident that a largely unarticulated, perhaps barely conscious discernment of class hierarchies combined with shrewd opportunism is brought to bear in order to secure educational advantage for their children.

Our feeling is that we're not interested in results, we're not interested in percentages of A–Cs, what we're interested in is what our own children are going to achieve. So it could be that a year group do appallingly, but if the teachers have given our children the opportunity to rise to their natural place and get the qualifications that they're capable of, a good teacher will work with children and if they have one bright child in that class they should be able to take them where they need to go. (Alison, white, middle-class parent)

Here again a middle-class parent is clear that her children will be having very different educational experiences, with very different educational outcomes to the working-class children who attend the same school. Such sentiments were widespread and, frequently fulfilled, as the following quotes make clear.

The funny thing is, something I didn't realise is, I think it is very good for their self-esteem, I mean we are free-loading in a way, partly because they have got all these opportunities and a lot of them are cheap and/or free, but also they are top of the tree academically at a school like that and if they went to another school they would be average ... But I think they think they are great, and so that is very good for their self-esteem. (Sally, white, middle-class parent, London)

Bryony has come out very confident because she was top of the pile as well in that school and she overcame all her fears and worries at the beginning and has come out extremely well adjusted socially and emotionally, very confident and knows where she wants to go. (Julian, white, middle-class parent, London)

Julian goes on to point out that although it has been difficult for his daughter at times, she has learnt important skills that will stand her in good stead later in the labour market, as 'she will have learnt what makes kids like that tick and how to deal with them'. Rather than developing any empathetic understanding, the challenge is to learn about and understand the working-class as a problem to be dealt with. Joan, a parent living in the North East, expresses similar condescension laced with distaste and pity:

I go into school frequently as a governor and I see horrendous children, children that you think what is going to happen to them? Where are they going to go? And my poor children who are really nice have to be in among them. (Joan, white, middle-class parent)

The key distinction here is between 'nice' middle-class children and 'horrendous' working-class ones. Regardless of 150 years of universal state education the working classes continue to be positioned within the educational system as an unknowing, unreflexive, tasteless mass from which the middle-class draw their distinction. Despite these families' left-leaning, communitarian impulses, most had complex and difficult feelings towards their working-class other, ranging from Joan's visceral distaste to more ambivalent but still defended responses.

This language of being 'top of the pile', and the class segregation that underpins it, was reinforced by what the young people told us. Davina, one of the white, middle-class students told us, "It's good because if you are in set one you know you are top of the pile", while Ollie joked "the top sets are chav free". Ironically, given the many fears and anxieties of their parents, the middle-class children who remain in non-selective state secondary schools nearly all experienced a class-segregated education in the top sets. This language of 'top of the pile' clearly indicates a sense of superiority that processes of setting and streaming build upon and encourage. But if the middle classes are to be, in their own words 'top of the pile' and 'top of the tree academically', someone else needs to be at the bottom. The assumption of the vast majority of the middle-class parents is that this is perfectly natural and to be expected. But the question I want to ask is, 'is it fair?'

The natural 'brightness' of the middle-class child is constantly juxtaposed to the dullness of the working-class majority. So it is predictable that the middle classes predominate in the top sets, monopolise scarce resources (a majority of the middle-class children in the study had been in gifted and talented groups). Of course this is not segregated education in the sense of separate private education, but it is still segregated education as most of the middle-class children made clear when they pointed out that they had little contact with the working classes after the first year and their friends nearly all came from the same class background as themselves. Despite all the parents expressing the importance of social mixing with those from different class and ethnic backgrounds, the vast majority (over 90%) of the white, middle-class young people were firmly and primarily anchored in white, middle-class social groups. Parents expressed varying degrees of concern about this, from Isabel's surprised tone about the lack of diversity in her son's friends, to Alicia's matter-of-fact acceptance.

Andrew has stuck with exactly the same friends as he had at primary school. I think it's extraordinary, I've tried to say invite people back ... but they're all from families like us, they're always from white middle-class families. (Isabel, white, middle-class parent)

Now my particular friendship group didn't change because I was running with the university-bound high achievers, the debate team and things like that. There weren't too many of those sorts of kids who came from those inner-city estates. There were some because I mean kids will achieve despite their setting sometimes. But no, not my immediate friendship group. (Alicia, white, middle-class student)

The words and the practices of these white, middle-class families resonate with Julienne Ford's findings 50 years ago.[6] She found that the comprehensive school failed to neutralise the impact of social class on children's friendship patterns.

Mike Savage argues that 'the unacknowledged normality of the middle classes needs to be carefully unpicked and exposed'.[7] The natural, taken-for-granted brightness of the middle classes also needs to be challenged, and particularly the assumption that it is natural and intrinsic rather than carefully constructed and intensively nurtured from birth, something that Annette Lareau calls the 'concerted cultivation' of the middle-class.[8]

I think what was really important to us was that the school had made provisions for the fact that Amelia was a bright kid. So whether they chose to do that by setting and streaming or whether they had classroom assistants or whatever, as long as they were supporting her to her full potential that was important. And the school does stream and they're put in forms according to their SATs results in primary school and she's in that top class. And they are also doing gifted and talented programme with her as well so that's been fantastic. But just having that kind of encouragement and pushing her that little bit makes all the difference. Of course

she gets that at home, but it's good she gets it at school as well.
(White, middle-class mother, London)

Here we see Amelia's brightness being 'pushed' and 'encouraged' both at school and at home. At school she is in the top sets and gifted and talented classes, while at home her parents pay for private tuition as well as music, sports and drama classes. We gain a sense that her potential may well be being realised. But this raises philosophical and moral issues as to whether supporting some children in realising their potential and not others is ethical. Of course the English educational system has always worked in this way, set up not to realise the potential of all children but only the select few. The objective of many upper- and middle-class parents is to ensure that their children are educational winners, but not all children can be winners and the provision of an educational system that caters for winners also reinforces and solidifies the position of losers. There is a long-standing, common-sense belief that we cannot all succeed academically. And if we did, what counts now as educational success would lose its value. So the working classes become a form of 'educational collateral damage' that ensures the success of their privileged class 'others'.

We get a sense of the working classes as educational 'collateral damage' in what white, middle-class Camilla says about class differences in her multi-ethnic state secondary school in London.

I think the working-class kids looked up to me to a certain extent and I didn't sort of consciously think it but I subconsciously felt slightly superior to them in that I had everything that they didn't have. You know, everything that my mum and dad had given me, and I was more intelligent than they were and there was more going for me than there was for them. (Camilla, white, middle-class student, London)

Here we are also presented with the pervasive middle-class sense of intellectual superiority. I have already referred to the perceived brightness of the middle-class child. In the 250 interviews we conducted there were 254 allusions to 'being bright', all references to white, middle-class students and their friends. This monopolising of 'brightness' by the middle-class within state schooling yet again positions the working-class across ethnicity as the 'lesser other' within educational systems. But this 'brightness' is often cultivated, manufactured, sometimes even coerced by a significant number of middle-class parents who are over-anxious and powerfully invested in their children's educational excellence.

Nowhere is this more evident than in the exponential increase in private tuition since the beginning of the 21st century. When I first wrote about private tuition in 2002 I was attacked for bias and exaggeration. In a study of 454 Year 6 London children Helen Lucey and I found that private tutoring was the norm for middle-class children.[9] In one predominantly middle-class primary school 65% of 11-year-olds were being tutored. A significant minority of their parents spent over £100 a week on tutoring – more than many of the families in the working-class schools we were researching in had to living on. As Jenni Russell wrote at the time:

> Three years ago, a quarter of the 11-year-olds at one high-achieving north London primary school were being tutored. Last year, it was one-third. This year, it's half. At another, lower-scoring school nearby, one-sixth of the top year were being tutored three years ago; this year, the number has doubled. A third school has just two middle-class children. Each has a tutor.[10]

Since then, the boom in private tuition has continued apace. A 2016 report from the Sutton Trust found that across England and Wales about 25% of all state-educated 11- to 16-year-olds have received private tuition at one time or another, rising to 42% in London – a rise of 18% since 2006.[11] The study also found that privately educated students were twice as likely to receive private tuition as were state-educated students. This relentless quest for educational advantage is matched by the ceaseless pursuit of distinction and culture. Carol Vincent and her colleagues write about the 'making up of the middle class child', in which they describe middle-class children's participation from a very young age in a range of commercial, often expensive enrichment activities that often left them with little free time. They argue that this process of constant stimulation is about competition and accruing advantage.[12]

Maintaining middle-class advantage in mixed-class classrooms

The following extract is from one of three interviews with Frankie, a white, middle-class girl in a working-class school. It exemplifies the issues of middle-class educational advantage, but also a very different but increasingly undervalued advantage that comes from mixing with those who are very different to oneself.

Frankie: *But the funny thing is, and I'm not trying to be silly, we've got some posh people in our class and if you are posh you are more clever.*

Diane: *Why would that be, Frankie?*

Frankie: *If you've got the money you get the most education.*

Diane: *You mean their mums and dads pay for their education?*

Frankie: *No. I mean you've got the most amount of time. Like, I have lots of support from my like mum and dad, like when I come home they are like – they are really ... Sometimes they are bit too enthusiastic (...) Like, did you get any maths homework today? OK let's do it right now.*

Diane: *So do you think it's got a lot to do with your family and the support your family give you?*

Frankie: *Yeah, definitely, because people like Jack isn't ... he's not very bright because I don't think he's got supportive parents. Well, it's not that he's not got a supportive family, necessarily, but he's a very, just not a very enthusiastic learner because of his background.... I mean, sometimes my parents are like ... did you get any homework? And they always like, go over it with you, and if you are having any troubles, or like, I don't understand this, they are like – oh I'll explain it to you ...*

Diane: *So some people get lots more help?*

Frankie: *Some people, at first, they start school not very bright and lots of people are ahead of them, and then they've got a little chance to catch up but they just think – what's the point? I'm never going to catch up with these people they are too far ahead. They could catch up a little bit, but they are just like – what's the point? I'm never going to catch up.*

In this extract Frankie, a nine-year-old white, middle-class girl, displays a keen awareness of class differences in education and why many working-class children give up on the intense and unfair competition that education has become. First, they have to contend with the common belief, which Frankie shares, that they are less intelligent than their upper- and middle-class peers. She also succinctly captures the double bind of working-class children, already behind their upper- and middle-class counterparts by the time they start school. Even if they manage to marshal sufficient self-belief and feelings of self-worth to challenge pervasive views that they are 'not very bright', they then find themselves in a race for educational success in which the upper and middle classes have started at least half way round the track, propelled forward by help from confident experts – either their parents or, if they are too busy, paid tutors. Although Frankie makes a distinction between time and money, asserting that middle-class children benefit from their parents' attention and engagement with their schooling, what she does not reveal, but her mother told me in a later interview, is that Frankie has been having paid tuition in English and Maths since she was seven. But at least Frankie is in a diverse, mixed classroom, and there is one working-class girl in her top set, the Tigers. In a later interview Frankie tells me that Leanne is brilliant at art – 'she can draw like a grown up' – and that 'she is one of the best creative writers in the class'. Many of the children in Frankie's class made a distinction between the 'posh' and the 'povs', both demonised groups because the poshies parade their privilege while the povs have no means of covering up their poverty. Frankie is a poshie who manages to evade the label by acting 'streetwise', but Leanne, growing up in a lone-mother family on benefits and living on a council estate, has little chance of escaping the 'pov' label. Yet Frankie's close-up experience of children who are very different from her has taught her that 'povs' are not all the same; some, like Leanne, can be and are clever while remaining resolutely working class. Segregated education of all complexions, from private schools to grammar schools, does not allow for this experience of mixing between the social classes. The very few working-class children in private schools, just like the very few working-class children in the top sets of grammar schools, have to either fade into the background and become invisibly working class or reinvent themselves as middle class.

I am going to draw briefly on two more empirical research projects, in order to further highlight relationality and the ways in which students experience a zero-sum game in which one child's educational success too often means another child's sense of educational failure. They also illustrate what I have called the psycho-social consequences of being working class in education: the ways in which wider social and economic injustices impact on working-class individuals' thoughts and feelings.[13] The two quotes below, both from working-class students, one in the US and the others in the UK, are infused with a potent sense of unfairness and unequal treatment.

Girl: *What I don't like about my school is how they treat us like animals, like they cage us up and like they keep putting more gates and more locks and stuff though they expect us to act like humans.*[14]

Martin: *Teachers look down on you.*

David: *Yeah, like they think you're dumb and stupid. We don't expect teachers to treat us like their own children. We're not. But we are still kids. I'd say to them, 'You've got kids. You treat them with love but you don't need to love us. All you need to do is treat us like humans.'*[15]

In both quotes we can see powerfully how the system of value that produces the middle-class as valuable, academic stars simultaneously generates a working class that is represented as incapable of having a self with value.[16] While entitlement and access to resources for making a self with value are central to how the middle classes are formed within education the consequence is too often a working class that is marginalised and seen to be without value. Class destinies in the 21st century remain tied to academic achievement. Furthermore, class has entered psychological categories as a way of socially regulating normativity and pathology within the educational field. However, although children expressed anxieties about school achievement across class differences, in the studies on which I am drawing it was not the white, middle-class boys panicking about being exposed as no good through school tracking, testing and assessment procedures. Rather, it was the black, and white, working-class girls agonising that they would be 'a nothing'.[17] Working-class students, like the girl in Michelle Fine and her colleagues' study, and the two boys in my UK study with Madeleine Arnot,[18] inhabit a psychic economy of class defined by fear, anxiety and unease where failure looms large and success is elusive, a space where they are positioned and see themselves as losers in the intense competition that education has become.

While there is an enduring quality to the elitism of the upper and the upper middle classes who send their children to private schools, the middle classes who send their children to state schools are facing new challenges that arise from a stagnant middle-class labour market and growing economic uncertainties. Middle-class relationships to education, while maintaining many common features with the past, have evolved in response to an increasingly competitive globalised labour market. The middle-class have had to engage in more and more academic, practical and emotional work in order to ensure their social advantage.[19] Middle-class relationships to schooling, particularly in the inner cities, have become characterised by high levels of anxiety. Here, as with the working-class, relationships to education have changed along with economic conditions. In particular, the premium put on educational credentials has grown as graduate jobs have diminished relative to the number of graduates.

As Andrew Sayer points out, part of the process of becoming moral subjects is by learning and acquiring behaviours and attitudes from others in our class settings.[20] When some sections of the middle classes opt for the private and selective state sector, parents like those in the study on the middle classes sending their children to urban comprehensives are often left with a sense of righteous indignation, but also anxiety and guilt. There is little access to the feelings of security that come from being part of a larger community of like-minded people. Instead we have a language of panic in which the psychological and emotional costs of principled choices become apparent. Unsurprisingly, anxiety, guilt and contradictory responses permeated our interviewees' responses. Cathy, a London mother, went to private school, as did her husband. She sent her two oldest children to private school before deciding to send Ben, her youngest, to the local comprehensive. In this quote we can see the powerful conscious and unconscious conflicts permeating Cathy's narrative, and gain a strong sense of the middle-class fear of contagion through contact with the working classes:

> They are very seductive, the private schools, they sort of, you know, into thinking they're the best and I think it's, yeah you could say it's racism it's classism at the start, but it's fear, it's fear that you're sending your child into a lesser environment, somewhere where they're not going to be able to do as well. (Cathy, white, middle-class mother)

Here Cathy indicates her awareness of prevalent middle-class fears that state comprehensives are in some way inferior. Such internal fears and defences are fuelled in the wider social world through discourses that themselves contain enduring fantasies about the inferior intellectual capacities of the working classes. Although she is clearly struggling against these perceptions, Cathy's 'lesser places' reveal 'the middle-class use of class as a defence, to create the illusion of superiority and false confidence, warding off fears of failure and inadequacy'.[21] We can see clearly a defence of status and distinction, and the ways in which the white middle classes, unproblematically in the instance of those sending their children to private schools, but in the case of these parents more conflictually, attempt to distinguish themselves as superior to others. What is also evident in the next quote is that the white middle-class do not view the majority working-class white and BME students in their schools as people whom they easily fit in with.

You know also he was the only, he was alone, he didn't have a single mate, he didn't know anybody, he was by himself, whereas virtually everybody else came up with a peer group, so he was sitting by himself and you know he is very white and he's very middle class. So looking round, all the groups are mixed, there isn't a sort of 'white middle-class group' he could go and slot himself into ... So I think he found it really difficult. I know he did, it was horrible, we used to walk to school and it was a nightmare. The first term I just felt sick, the whole time. I would like it to be the norm for people to go to their local school and not to be scared in the way that I was scared. I would like people like me to send their children to Broomwood and not be scared. I think a lot of my fear was irrational. I'm sure it was. I didn't even go and look at the school, so how rational can this be? (Cathy, white, middle-class mother)

Cathy, like many of the white, middle-class parents, expresses a great deal of ambivalence. At different points in the interview she talks about "the terrible terrible reputation of local state schools" and her sense of panic when considering them as possibilities for her own son. On the one hand, she projects her discomforts onto lesser people in lesser places, those through whom she can maintain her privileged status. But, on the other hand, she adopts a strong moral stance in relation to 'the good society' and asserts that if she wants society to be more fair, then she needs to act in certain ways, despite her fears. This tension between doing the best for one's own child and doing the best for wider society was there, to a greater or lesser extent, for all the parents. Yet again we glimpse internal conflicts and ambivalences. These parents were trying to behave ethically in a situation that is structurally unethical in terms of entrenched inequalities, and radically pluralistic in terms of different moralities and value systems.[22]

As a consequence, the routine nature of educational success and the apparent ease with which many middle-class children perform well academically masks deep fears around failure – fears that are driven underground because they threaten the very bases on which middle-class subjectivities are founded. But out of sight does not mean out of mind. It is precisely this level of terror about failure that lies behind the numerous strategies that many middle-class parents have for ensuring educational advantage for their children, strategies such as: insisting that the primary school curriculum prepare children for selective entrance exams; campaigning for setting and streaming to be introduced; employing private tutors; and buying properties within the catchment areas of high-achieving secondary schools (and when that latter strategy is too expensive, lying about addresses).

Tactics like these, although deriving from individual emotional processes, have had a significant impact in many localities on the educational market-place, serving to deepen already existing social class divisions in schooling. They are also so widespread as to constitute 'class action' although this kind of class action is not about transformation, but about reproduction. Also, although not often directly aimed at the working classes, they have a damaging impact on working-class educational opportunities. Middle-class children are learning an important lesson about failure: that it is intolerable, unwanted and belongs somewhere else. That is why contemporary educational policy is so paradoxical. It is nominally about raising working-class achievement, although its practices generate the exact opposite, ensuring that educational failure remains firmly located within the working classes. And part of that is because the middle classes do not want to take back those messy, expelled aspects of the self – fear, contempt, greed – because what would happen to their tenuous sense of centrality then? As Carolyn Steedman argues, it is the marginality of working-class stories that maintains the centrality of middle-class versions.[23] There is no kind of narrative that can hold the two together. Working-class accounts are always rendered outsiders' tales. How can it be otherwise when middle- and upper-class practices in the field of education add up to such powerful collective class action. Regardless of what individual working-class males and females are able to negotiate and achieve for themselves within education, the collective patterns of working-class trajectories remain sharply different from those of the upper and middle classes, despite 150 years of universal state schooling.

University: different worlds for different social classes

I have already looked at the very different experiences of the working, middle and upper classes at university in the last chapter. In this section I draw on my own experiences, as well as current research,[24] to illustrate how upper- and middle-class 'class action' works at university level to reinforce the position of working-class students as 'outsiders on the inside'. In their research examining the experiences of working-class students at a Russell Group university, Susan Coulson and her colleagues found that they were largely isolated. All, apart from one, had not joined any groups or societies. They talked of how disheartening and dispiriting they had found Freshers' Week, sometimes finding themselves friendless or in awkward social situations. My own experience 50 years earlier at the same university had similarly been disheartening, but also, at times, terrifying. I had applied to a number of halls of residence but was rejected by them all. One rejection letter blatantly stated that I would not fit in because I was from a different social background from the other students. I ended up being the only first-year female student to be placed in private lodgings; that my digs were three miles from the university further reinforced my isolation. I loved dancing, so was determined to go to the Freshers' Ball. A female medical student whose father had bought a flat for her in the same street as my student lodgings said she would give me a lift, although, like the working-class girl in Coulson et al's study, I was abandoned within five minutes of arriving, as she spotted a group of medics whom she knew, and darted off. Left to my own devices, I decided that the best approach was just to dance and try to enjoy myself. However, within a few minutes a group of young men, who I later learnt had been to a leading public school, approached me and asked if they had seen me earlier in Woolworths. The aspersion being cast was that I was an interloper, a local shop girl with no right to be there.

That negative encounter was the start of three troubled years. Coulson et al write that negative experiences during Freshers' Week signalled a failure to make friends that affected the working-class students' academic lives.

> They found many students were not necessarily interested in making friends with them and rejected their approaches. This could take the form of polite, but vague, interest followed by excuses; or in some cases, more privileged students' outright refusal to associate with those unlike themselves.[25]

I was never to become socially acceptable to the female middle-class students at my university, and failed to find another working-class female student. Instead, my female friends during the three years were a hairdresser and a secretary, both 'town' rather than 'gown'. I did, however, find that I was sexually acceptable to the middle- and upper-class male students. More perturbing was the sexual interest I attracted from my male lecturers. By the summer term of my first year I had been first propositioned and then sexually harassed by one of my sociology lecturers. When I went to see one of my tutors to ask for his help his suggestion was that we should go away for a weekend together in order to sort my problems out.

Coulson and her colleagues also write of the academic as well as the social difficulties faced by the working-class students in their study. One of the students spoke of hating to go to a lecture or seminar if they didn't have someone to walk in with. What I remember is the class prejudice and bigotry that permeated the curriculum. In one of the first lectures I attended the subject was working-class culture. The professor giving the lecture told the approximately 200 students present that coal miners kept their coal in the bath. While they wrote his words down I stood up, shouted rubbish and stormed out.

In a later lecture the same professor told us all that although he was a senior academic he would much prefer the joys of being a farm labourer, as they are in constant communication with nature and experience the pleasures of being in the open air. I had to leave for a second time. Soon afterwards attending seminars became increasingly difficult. My sociology lecturer suggested that I could talk in the sessions about the experience of being working class. He said it would be helpful for the other students who lacked experience of working-class lives. In his words, I 'could bring working-classness to life'. Instead, my first encounters with the middle and upper classes drained the life out of me. I became first anorexic, then bulimic, as I tried and failed to hold on to a bearable, authentic sense of self. What I want to convey here is that, far from university being the beginning of 'a new better middle-class life' for the working classes, as is often implied in the social mobility rhetoric, it is much more often another stage in a difficult and painful struggle to be accepted and included in middle-class contexts.

Conclusion

Relationality raises issues not only about the relationships between classes but also of how different aspects of identity coexist within class. At the most basic level class is always gendered and raced. This is evident in the extent to which girls across class express higher levels of anxiety about educational performance than boys do.[26] Of course there are other aspects of identity that cross-cut class. Social classes are intersected not only by gender, ethnicity, sexuality and dis/ability but also by differing class fractions. Relations differ widely in terms of how different groupings within the same class position themselves and are positioned by others, and in terms of how their relationships to education have evolved. So, to take one example, the white working-class have a different relationship to education to that of many BME working-class groups. While the white working-class often bring a collective memory of educational subordination and marginalisation to schooling, some BME groups in the global North bring histories of educational achievement in their countries of origin, although migration has often brought economic impoverishment and downward mobility. Others, despite a lack of educational credentials, bring a strong conviction that a fresh start in a new educational system will provide crucial opportunities for educational advancement that were denied to their parents. Yet other BME groups, such as the African

Caribbean in the UK, have, like their white, working–class peers, learnt to live with educational failure compounded, in their case, by racism. And these different ethnic groups are viewed very differently within white, middle–class imaginaries, with the white, working–class regularly ethnicised as too white and labelled as white trash,[27] while some minority ethnic groups, such as the Chinese and Indians, are singled out as the acceptable face of working–classness[28] – the so–called 'model minorities'.[29]

But the focus of this chapter has been the relationships between the different classes within education, and I want to come back to that. The working–class experience of education is not just one of being positioned as educational losers to middle–class educational successes but also one of being completely eclipsed by the 'shining stars' of the private schools. The consequences are a compounding of working–class educational neglect and marginalisation that results in a doubling of disadvantage as the working–class are relegated not just to second class but to the rank of third–class learners.

The middle classes have always been, and remain, the 'ideal learners' within state education. Yet they and the state system have always been in the shadow of the private school sector. The middle classes may be ideal learners, but the private school system has always been positioned as the ideal to which the state system should aspire and the snobbery and elitism underpinning the relationship between the two sectors has bedevilled state schooling, regardless of whether the system is a tripartite or a comprehensive one. English education is class divided. Of course there are fractions within the upper, middle and working classes, and flickerings and fluctuations at the boundaries of class divisions. But underlying these myriad internal class fractions, and movement at the edges, is a stark hierarchical divide between the upper, middle and working classes that has persisted throughout the history of English education.

In the next chapter I focus in more depth on the psychological pain and turmoil generated through class inequalities in education and draw out the emotional consequences of the unequal relationships between the different classes within schooling.

SEVEN

Class feeling: troubling the soul and preying on the psyche

Introduction

> There is another working class: what we might call
> the working class of the mind.[1]

This chapter focuses specifically on the emotional landscapes of class, showing how schools can become the source of all kinds of fantasies, fears, anxieties, hopes and desires. In particular, it attempts to expose the injuries of class that are perpetuated through the educational system. While the greatest damage is inflicted on the working classes, the chapter also draws on data to reveal the damage exacted on the middle and upper classes.

In earlier chapters we have seen repeatedly the ways in which classed experiences generate powerful emotional responses, from Steve McQueen's rage and disgust to the bottom-set students' shame and abjection. This chapter presents interview data collected between 2000 and 2015 to illustrate the powerful dynamic between emotions and class inequalities. Arguing that class is always lived on both a conscious and an unconscious level, it focuses on affective aspects of class, revealing the complicated combinations of guilt, shame, anger, fear, defensiveness, empathy and conciliation that are generated in response to class inequalities in education. In the first part of the chapter I draw on a number of case studies in order to illustrate the intense emotional pressure that results from attempting to succeed 'against the odds'. In the case of Shaun, the working-class boy, this pressure is caused by his working-class background; for Max, the middle-class boy, it is a consequence of context, the predominantly working-class comprehensive he attends. In the second part of the chapter I examine the powerful affective costs for working-class children of attending schools seen as being 'second rate' and 'low status' by both themselves and others.

Tales of trouble and turmoil

Shaun's story is of a hard-working, well-behaved, poor, white, working-class boy trying to achieve academically, first in a predominantly working-class, multi-ethnic primary school, then in a 'sink' inner-city boys' comprehensive school, while simultaneously trying to maintain his standing within the male peer-group culture.[2] And, despite his efforts and struggles, Shaun ended up leaving school at 16 with minimal qualifications. In order to understand Shaun's predicament I wanted to make sense of his psychic struggles as well as his educational trajectory; I wanted to understand how structures become embodied and generate ambivalences and tensions. Shaun's initial response to finding out that he is going to one of the most demonised schools in his local authority is a mixture of palpable fear and desperate search for remedies:

> ... all I know is that sometimes people sit and ask for 10p in Sutton Boys, because I've been finding out quite a lot about Sutton Boys because I am going there. So I am going to try and find out as much as I can about it, because if I don't and I go into school and people go – have you seen something or so and so? And then they are going to pull you into the toilets and beat you up. So if I find out all about it I'll know how to protect myself from the rough kids. (Shaun, white, working-class boy)

But Shaun's tale also speaks to the difficulty that haunts many early school-leavers – that of managing movement across two different and at times opposing fields, those of the classroom and working-class peer-group culture.

Shaun: *Like now I am different in the class than I am out in the playground. I'm just different.*

Diane: *Right, so how are you different?*

Shaun: *In the playground, yeah, in the classroom, should I say, I am not myself, I'm totally different. I am hard working and everything. Out in the playground, yeah, I am back to my usual self, wanting to fight and everything, just being normal. Like, when I'm in my school uniform I think – I don't want to fight no more, because I don't want to crease my uniform or whatever.*

However, there is also a great deal of struggle and conflict. Shaun's narrative illustrates the difficulties of reconciling white, working-class masculinities with educational success in inner-city working-class schooling. And we see throughout his narrative that combining the two generates heavy psychic costs, involving him not only in an enormous amount of academic labour but also in an intolerable burden of psychic reparative work. Bourdieu uses the metaphor of fish in water, those who are able to take the world around them for granted, swimming without having to consider how to swim.[3] Shaun's tale is one of floundering rather than swimming, of being weighted down rather than weightless. He is positioned in an untenable space on the boundaries of two irreconcilable ways of being and has to produce an exhausting body of psychic, intellectual and interactive work in order to maintain his contradictory ways of being, his dual perception of self. He is continually engaged in a balancing act that requires superhuman effort, maintaining his status in his working-class male peer group while attempting to succeed academically. We gain a sense of how blurred the lines are between psychic processes and social processes. The position in which Shaun finds himself is one of struggle between two conflicting social pressures, where his loyalties are tugged and pulled in different directions. In Shaun's quote we have a clear example of the turmoil working-class children can face when caught between two very different but equally compelling pressures, and the ensuing internal conflict. Shaun is situated at a point where the contradictions between white, working-class, male solidarity and the neoliberal impetus to self-improvement and academic excellence are painfully apparent. This resulted in a heightened emotional sensitivity in order to cope with such conflicts.

But by the end of the first year at secondary school, the two conflicting aspects of identity that Shaun has put so much effort into reconciling are beginning to fall apart:

> It's getting much harder because like some boys, yeah, like a couple of my friends, yeah, they go 'Oh, you are teacher's pet' and all that. But I have to do my work but I don't want to fall out with my mates, I want to stay friends with my mates. (Shaun, white, working-class boy)

The double bind inscribed in Shaun's educational enterprise has led to a self divided against itself. Intense loyalty to class and community is at odds with individual striving for success. Shaun has to engage in a punishing process of self-regulation in the face of his desires to be 'one of the boys'. The effort of reconciling these tensions had taken its toll and was revealed in Shaun's longing to be a baby again:

> I want to stay younger, like I wish I was younger now. So I wouldn't have to move, just sleep in my cot and have no responsibility. But you've got to get older. You can't just stay the same age. (Shaun, white, working-class boy)

Evident in Shaun's words is the suffering that can be generated when working-class children and young people feel torn by contradictions and internal divisions.

> Some boys, yeah, in English yeah, some of the kids never shut up, never, ever shut up. Like, today, we were supposed to get out for lunch at ten past one, because all the bigger kids push in front of us, but because everyone was shouting and everything and I am the one that always goes – shut up, behave. So whenever I tell them to shut up they are scared of me and they shut up, but then this boy Ryan he always comes back and says something, so we have to stay in. He always pushes it. They all show off. Because Jay, yeah, this year, I think he's had more fights than he did out

of all the time at Beckwith, so far, because like, today, yeah, that boy Ryan picked up a chair and Jay stood on the table and flying kicked the chair into the kid's face and then punched him and he fell back on the floor. And, like, David is encouraging him. He was going – go on, Jay, go over there and punch him in his face. And when they were fighting and everyone was going – go on, Jay, go on, Jay. They can't just sit down and ignore it or try and break it up. And I just got sick of it cos I'm the only one trying to get on with my work. (Shaun, white, working-class boy)

For Shaun, they were throwing their lives away, but it must also have felt to him that they were throwing his life away too. Lynsey Hanley, writing of Willis's (1997) working-class lads, comments that 'the cost of one of them saying "come on lads, we can have a laff outside of school, we're here to learn so we don't have to do jobs we hate later on" would have been too much for any one of them to stand'.[4] But that was exactly what Shaun was attempting and failing to do.

Throughout the four interviews I conducted with Shaun while he was at secondary school, a complex, and at times contradictory, interweaving of ambivalence, defensiveness and pride were evident.

Sutton Boys isn't the best school in the area but it ain't the worst. I'd say it's like in the middle. Yeah, not good or bad, like medium, well sometimes a bit bad especially when there are fights, but not always. We have some very good teachers and you can get on with your work if you try.... Other kids diss it, say it's full of tramps, but they don't really know what it's like. (Shaun, white, working-class boy)

In the last interview he told me:

I don't know what to do about my mates. They just muck about all the time. I tell Jay to stop but he just says I am a wuss and to stop sucking up to the teacher. I'm exhausted trying to keep it all together. (Shaun, white, working-class boy)

Here, and in the earlier quote about wanting to be a baby again, we see the heavy psychological toil that managing the two conflicting demands exerts on Shaun. His resolve is being stretched to the limit as he attempts to reconcile the increasingly irreconcilable. In the end the struggle between educational success and working-class peer-group pressure became too much, and Shaun left school at 16 when all his friends left. There are two key points about the educational context that it is important to draw out. First, Shaun's school was over 95% working class, with 47% of children on FSM. If he withdrew from his mates there was no one left to be friends with. Focusing on academic work and spurning his friends meant social isolation, a big ask for a gregarious 14-year-old. Second, like many other comprehensives in the area, the school had a huge staff turnover and large numbers of supply teachers. This was highlighted in an Ofsted report at the time. So, Shaun could not replace reliance on his friends with reliance on the teachers; they were never there long enough. As he said mournfully at the end of his first year at Sutton Boys, "You never know who you are going to get. We've had four maths teachers so far this year." Then, the following year:

We've had lots of different teachers this year in science and French. French is worst. We've had five teachers in one term and when a new one comes whatever you've learnt before they teach us again. And sometimes they will go too far and we ain't even on the first step so it's very confusing. (Shaun, white, working-class boy)

Shaun's account of high teacher turnover fits with the research. In 2012 Allen et al found a positive association between the level of school disadvantage and the turnover rate of its teachers. They also found that poorer schools were hiring much younger teachers, on average.[5] It is not only common-sense views about white, working-class masculinities that are unsettled by Shaun's story. His narrative allows us glimpses into the moral vacuum that stands for current 'common sense' educational thinking. We can see in his account how educational processes help class exclusions to operate.[6] Shaun's struggle against the educational context he finds himself in is yet one more instance of the myth of comprehensivisation and the sham of meritocracy. Political parties of all hues lash out against 'bog standard comprehensives',[7] yet schools like Sutton Boys do not have, and have never had, a comprehensive intake. As a previously 'failing' school that has just come out of 'special measures', both the school and its predominantly working-class, ethnic minority intake are demonised both locally and within the wider public imagination.[8] Unlike the fantasies played out in educational policies, this is not an issue of school effectiveness and school leadership but a matter of class and race inequalities, of social structures and material resources.

Furthermore, despite the much-vaunted National Curriculum, our politicians and policy makers appear to have no interest in what counts as 'really useful knowledge' for working-class students.[9] As Jackie Brine asserts, the continued failure to critically educate and to creatively stimulate working-class students is little short of criminal and, at the very least, morally indefensible.[10] Even Shaun, with his strong commitment to learning, finds most of what he is taught an irrelevance. His disaffected working-class peers at Sutton, as well as contemporaries in other inner-city schools, find little to engage them in the National Curriculum.[11] Perhaps it is worth revisiting Basil Bernstein's counsel of more than 45 years ago in order to radically rethink socially equitable education for all class groupings in society. He argued that we must ensure that the material conditions of the schools we offer, their values, social organisation, forms of control and pedagogy, the skills and sensitivities of the teachers are refracted through an understanding of the culture the children bring to the school. As he pointed out, we do no less for the middle-class child.[12]

The affinity and affection that I felt for Shaun were unexpected. Although I really empathised with his situation, it was never mine. I was not torn between getting on and staying put. I genuinely thought that I could do both: achieve educationally and remain at the heart of my family and community. It didn't work out that way, but at the time I was so preoccupied with doing as well as the headmaster's son and, later, when I was at secondary school, the doctor's daughter that most other aspects of school life paled into insignificance. As a working-class girl in a middle-class school I was never popular, but I can't remember caring too much. What I do remember is my exam scores.

I want to compare and contrast Shaun's story with that of Max, to look at psychic conflicts being managed by a very different young man. Max, a white, middle-class student in an ethnically diverse, predominantly working-class South London comprehensive, was, by the beginning of year 10, one of a handful of white, middle-class boys in his year group. He explained how he dealt with the tensions between high achievement and a working-class peer group.

I did my own thing but with lots of support and like, yeah, I was never held back and I was always really pushed by my teachers. In class things I always felt a bit uncomfortable because I would always be kind of straining myself from sounding like a twat (laughs). But in general I was allowed to write like a twat in my books and I just got on with it. I am not saying I found things easy it was just that I compelled myself to do more than anyone else did. Like I just worked longer, it's kind of like a neurosis. (Max, white, middle-class boy)

In the quote Max articulates clearly a boundary-drawing process that separates him off from his working-class peer group. He hints at some of the costs in this process, explaining that he "didn't want to stand out as the sad nerd" and he always had "to be careful not to piss the other kids off". However, his father, himself from a working-class background, makes the costs explicit, when he explains why Max dropped out of a gifted and talented leadership programme:

Anyway they wanted three kids for this gifted and talented leadership scheme and he was chosen for one of them and I remember him coming home and saying "oh great". And the next day he was just crying for no reason at all and so they took him to the office and it happened again. And so they took him to the doctor and they arranged a visit, it was amazing, within a week with the educational psychologist. And then we got six sessions with him and me almost straightaway and it turns out that I had

been putting too much pressure on him and that was the last straw.
(Father of Max, white, middle-class boy)

Both son and father were managing, or rather failing to manage,
an unbearable amount of conflict and divided loyalties. Here
again, as we saw in Shaun's case, there is intense psychological
stress as Max collapses under the pressure of attempting, and
failing, to reconcile the pursuit of academic excellence with
fitting into a working-class, multi-ethnic peer group.

Yet the double bind that Max and his family are negotiating
is very different from that facing Shaun. Max is nominally
middle class but, as always with social class, it is never quite that
straightforward. Both Max's parents grew up in working-class
families, were teachers and lived in local authority housing.
Talking about his background, Max's father said:

> *My four grandparents came over as children, all Irish. My father
> was a bus driver and all my uncles were dockers or steel workers
> or shipbuilders. I had one uncle who was a ticket clerk on the
> railway, that was the highest we got. And the women didn't work,
> my mother never worked, she worked in service for about two years
> before she got married. They both left school at 14 and so it was
> very working class.* (Father of Max, white, middle-class boy)

It is unsurprising, then, that despite identifying as middle
class, Max's parents still expressed a great deal of ambivalence
about actually being middle class. Max's mother reasoned that
"while my loyalties are mostly working class I'd have to own
up to being middle class because I've got a good job with good
pay". Her comment speaks volumes about perceptions of the
status and value of working-class jobs in contemporary Britain,
but it also reveals the difficult tensions she is trying to manage
between emotional attachments and objective position. Max's
father also uncovers similar strains. Speaking of the ethically and
economically diverse area the family lived in, he commented:

> *I am completely embedded in this community in the sense that it
> is two worlds really. I am the secretary of the Tenants' Association
> here and the Tenants' Association's totally working class, and I am*

chair of the Community Association, which is all the nobs and very middle class, and I am sort of straddling the two, just about. (Father of Max, white, middle-class boy)

Max's father's use of the term 'straddling' is apposite; that is exactly what the family are attempting to do – straddle two classes in order not to lose a sense of connection with where they have come from. But when I asked where he himself was positioned on his spectrum of belonging and not belonging, he laughed and said "that's a hard one".

The white middle classes who live here on the whole don't really invest in the local area, mostly it's just somewhere they live rather than somewhere they belong, and the vast majority wouldn't dream of sending their kids to the local school. It's different for the working-class families on our estate, they do have a sense of belonging. (Father of Max, white, middle-class boy)

Parents like Max's are dealing with the contradiction of trying to act for the common good in a deeply individualistic, competitive education market. Their commitment to comprehensive schooling and a fairer educational system conflicts with their desire for their children to both get the best and be the best.

In the same study that Max was part of, on the white middle-classes sending their children to urban comprehensives, Camilla, in her mid-20s, was the most transparent about the difficult feelings that class differences can arouse. When we interviewed her she reflected on how, when she was at secondary school, "there was an element of being embarrassed about being middle class". Her recollections of her secondary school experiences illuminated difficult tensions between empathy and desires to distance herself. Once again the ambivalences and tensions that characterised many of these middle-class individuals' attitudes to their working-class others were evident. On the one hand, she expressed pity and compassion:

I was quite upset to see it though, and I remember feeling really sorry for them because although I knew it happened and I knew it was an issue, you know, until you actually see it for yourself you don't actually think about it. And then knowing that we had so much more and knowing that when I came back after my first day my mum was going to ask me how it went. And there were so many kids there whose parents obviously probably didn't have hardly anything and, you know, weren't going to ask or didn't care sort of thing, and that was quite sad. (Camilla, white, middle-class woman)

However, permeating her sense of empathy, and embarrassment at her own privilege, was a countervailing sense of superiority. Her words also poignantly reveal her need to defend against a sense of inferiority in relation to her parents, who are both senior academics.

And I think also because my mum and dad had achieved so much I think I probably felt quite second rate to them, and being friends with these people made me feel like the one, you know, who was achieving, you know, and was superior to them. (Camilla, white, middle-class woman)

What was apparent in Camilla's words, and more widely across the sample, was a powerful defence mechanism against privileged circumstances. It was most evident in the claiming of brightness, which underpinned the parents' rationalisation that they deserved the best for their children, and provided a justification for monopolising scarce educational resources. Freud argued that when faced with a traumatic situation that calls into question one's integrity, the ego often deals with what appears to be an irreconcilable dilemma through processes of disavowal that lead to a splitting of the ego.[13] There is simultaneously both a denial of class privilege and a protection of it. But, as Lynn Layton argues:

> the haunting anxiety about necessity remains and must be vigilantly guarded against; dependency, lack of agency, relationality and connection to others must be repudiated.[14]

In schools where the white middle classes have to confront poverty, need, deprivation, and an evident neglect by state and educational institutions to deal with them, the result is enormous middle-class ambivalence, the empathy that Camilla portrays, but also potent defences and defensiveness that increase rather than reduce the social distances between the classes.

What I am struggling to grasp here are the psychic consequences of the relationship between economic inequalities and social class. Economic inequalities take shape psychically for all individuals through binaries of middle and working class, rich and poor. But, as Sarah Smart's research shows, it is easier to deal with divisions between rich and poor rather than with class divisions, because they leave out the middle-class self. But a desire to be outside the class system, and a denial that class has any importance in contemporary society, does not equate with transcending and rising above either the class system or the inequalities that underpin it. Rather, by claiming to be in the middle people can talk about inequalities without feeling personally implicated either as those who, in lacking resources, are seen to be intrinsically lacking or as those with resources who can be viewed as selfish and greedy. It is unsurprising, then, that nearly everyone asserts that they are in the middle, or, as Mike Savage et al found, claim to be 'ordinary'.[15] This appears to add another layer of complication to the messy issue of class identity. But perhaps the high percentage of the middle-class who insist on claiming a working-class identity, particularly if they come from working-class backgrounds, primarily want to avoid being associated with privilege, individualism and self-seeking. But while the evidence from my research projects powerfully suggests that everyone is damaged by the social class inequalities that continue to haunt the educational system, it is important to reiterate that it is the working classes who suffer the most. Shaun does not have the opportunity to realise his potential, while Max does. In the next section of the chapter I examine the emotional consequences for working-class children of being relegated to schools that both others and they themselves see as 'rubbish' and 'no good'.

'Rubbish' schools for 'rubbish' children

The painful accounts of working-class children reveal the class inequalities that lie at the heart of parental choice. The children's narratives were full of metaphors of 'waste', 'refuse' and 'rejection'.

> *That school is shit, y'know man [referring to Deerpark].* (Kardel, black, working-class boy)

> *You have had it if you go to Chiltern, it's for no-hopers* (Jessie, white, working-class girl)

In these accounts demonised schools became repositories for 'stupid' and 'thick' students, the ones that good schools did not want. Working-class children were acutely aware of the hierarchy of selection in terms of cleverness, and nearly always had a painfully accurate idea of where they themselves were positioned in the ranking. They were having to deal with the powerful assaults to the self that came with going to schools that others thought were not good enough for intelligent people.

A lot of the working-class young people talked in terms of trying to stay 'normal' in the pathologised schools they were moving to. So Maria said "I'll try and stay normal even though Chiltern is a bad school", while Joe agonised about the dilemma he faced:

> *If I went to Chiltern I would probably get a bit, uhm, I'm not saying everyone that goes there is bad, but I might get a bit argumentative with everyone and get into fights, starting fights and all that, get into trouble. But in Westbury I think I'll just be normal, stay the same ... so I have to try and be like I'd be in Westbury but in Chiltern.* (Joe, white, working-class boy)

However, it is Lewis's tale that exemplifies the psychological repercussions of the struggle to remain normal and avoid pathologisation. Lewis, working class and Black British, realises that he is likely to be allocated a place in a demonised school.

His brother attended Chiltern, but his mother was unhappy about Lewis joining him there and put down Westbury as first choice. She told me: "it has had a very disruptive effect on Perry's education. They don't seem to be able to keep a teacher for more than five minutes. They all leave almost as soon as they get there." Of course, Lewis and Perry's mother is exaggerating, but the statistics on teacher turnover in working-class urban comprehensives indicate that she has a point. Lewis was refused a place at Westbury on the grounds of distance, and after an unsuccessful appeal was, after all, placed in Chiltern.

In the interview Lewis had a number of conflicting knowledges to draw on: his brother's direct experience of the school – itself a mixed experience; his mother's anxious feelings about the school; educational league table data; and the general agreement among his peers that this is a bad school.

> *Well, with Chiltern it was kind of good and bad because I knew my brother went there and he had made loads of friends, but I was just a bit worried about the people in there, the bullying and because my brother told me that Chiltern has the worst SATs results in the whole of Ashbury borough. But I think, and I've said this to my bigger brother, I think that there are more bullies in Chiltern than there are in any other school in Ashbury … the other kids have wound me up, they're all saying Chiltern is just for thick kids.* (Lewis, black, working-class boy)

Lewis's attempts to feel OK about his situation are undermined by the pervasive view among his peer group that, in the words of Adam, his best friend, Chiltern "is a rubbish school for rubbish kids". In fact, the only easily verifiable fact about Chiltern – that it has the "worst SATs results in the whole of Ashbury borough" – itself contradicts another layer of subjective knowledge based on his brother's performance:

> Lewis: *They're [his parents] all right about it, because they see my brother Perry and they see that he's worked out OK, he's doing good in his GCSEs, so they want me to go there. But because my mum's seen Westbury as a really good school as well, she thinks*

it's better than Chiltern, so she put it as first choice, that's why.
(Lewis, black, working-class boy)

But then again, Lewis has to deal with the peer group consensus that Chiltern is "just for thick kids". Going to schools like Chiltern is not just about being seen to be 'bad' it is also about being 'stupid'. For working-class children the shame and humiliation of being thought of as stupid is ever present. In the wider middle-class imagination the feared or reviled parts of the self are projected onto demonised schools, their students, teachers and the communities they serve, while there is an idealisation of schools that are seen to cater for the 'bright' and successful. The consequences for the ethnically diverse, working-class children attending such schools is that they are left to deal with the pain of being pathologised, and the threats to a positive sense of self that such pathologisation entails. Although it is clear that working-class children's experiences of going to demonised schools are not all the same, there is no getting away from the emotional repercussions of being positioned at the bottom of the educational market, in schools in the lower reaches of local authority league tables. The ways in which working-class schools and their students come to be demonised are a powerful example of how the choice process operates as a form of social class exclusion.

In actuality, the working-class children who were most likely to go to demonised schools had both positive and negative experience of, knowledge about and feelings towards them, as we saw in Chapter Four. In the group discussion where other children recounted more and more horrific stories about Chiltern, the fragile positive feelings that Lewis struggled to sustain began understandably to crumble. At one point he said, "I don't want to get into Chiltern, after I've just heard all this". Amazingly, however, he managed to hang on in there, forever hopeful that it needn't be like that for him, holding on to a version of a future reality in which he could somehow remain himself.

There's this boy called Taylor, he's in Year 8 and he hasn't got into any fights. He hasn't done anything wrong yet. So I'm just hoping

I can be like him and just stay as I normally am, and nothing will happen. (Lewis, black, working-class boy)

We could understand Lewis's last comments as wishful, a rather desperate attempt at the kind of magical thinking that will make everything all right. For working-class children like Lewis attending schools at the bottom of local authority league tables, the struggle to separate out from the demonised other when it is conflated with the self generates painful social and psychological consequences that the upper and middle classes do not have to face. And, like Shaun, whom I have discussed earlier, it proves impossible for Lewis to stay 'good' and successful in an educational context that is widely seen to be a place of failure.

When I interviewed Lewis and his mother for the last time, at the end of Lewis's second year at Chiltern, both displayed a mixture of sad resignation and fragile hopes for something better. Both complained about the frequent disruption of teaching, particularly in maths, science and computing, because of the regular turnover of teachers in these subject areas. But the main topic of conversation was Lewis's deteriorating behaviour in school. His mother, visibly desperate about how to help Lewis, spoke despairingly about her efforts to support him. She told how at various times she had withdrawn his pocket money, stopped him going out in the evening to play football and initiated a reward chart that was still pinned to the kitchen wall as we spoke. Lewis, clearly ashamed, alternated between a defiant defensiveness and sorrowful appeasement. The teachers didn't like him, some were even racist, the work was really boring, he was either in a higher set where the work was too hard or a lower set where the work was too easy. In response to his mother's entreaty that he had to keep his head down and work hard, he remonstrated that that was impossible with work that was so uninteresting and a peer group that would mock him. In these difficult circumstances both Lewis and his mother clung to the faltering hope that if he could only go to a better school it would all be better. The overriding impression I was left with at the end of the interview was of the impossibility of both mother's and son's position.

Angst and anxiety in school choice

So far I have focused primarily on the emotional tensions faced by students; in the next section I look at the case study of a middle-class mother dealing with the emotional turmoil caused by choice of school. Middle-classness traditionally has been about containment and restraint; in fact these qualities are part of the reason why the middle-class have come to represent the social and educational ideal. Rather, it is the working-class who have always been portrayed as repositories for excessive emotion.[16] However, in all my research it is clear that the middle classes experience intense emotional conflicts and tensions in relation to their children's schooling. This seepage is often most visible in the narratives of those middle-class from working-class backgrounds, and below I discuss Yvonne, a working-class girl who became a middle-class mother.

Yvonne was a coal miner's daughter before becoming a dancer and marrying a middle-class man. When her oldest daughter went to Copethorpe comprehensive it was bottom of the local authority league table with 17% A★–C grades at GCSE. Throughout her interview Yvonne reiterates her deep commitment to comprehensivisation, but this strong commitment is in constant tension with her fear of the consequences of acting on her belief.

> *I was totally freaked out by the whole prospect of secondary school and all Tanya's friends went to Dearham Park and I thought I was like minded with these mothers, but it wasn't until the secondary school thing I thought no, they are not, and I was panicking about it and Tanya wanted to go to Dearham Park. She said her friends were picking their school and why couldn't she pick hers. I said Tanya, they are not picking their school, their mum is picking their school and if you go to Dearham Park, their mum will have picked your school too. I said I don't believe in segregation of any kind, whether it is single sex, faith schools, fee paying, whatever people do to divide us, and I wholeheartedly mean that and so you have to go to a mixed school with no special faith where there is a mixture of kids, and this is our local mixed school.* (Yvonne, white, middle-class mother)

The calm, reasoned explanation Yvonne provides to Tanya belies her panicked, anxious feelings about school choice. In many ways Yvonne is one of the least ambivalent of the parents. She is passionately committed to comprehensive schooling and told me that "there is no way I'd move my kids. I think it is the responsibility of parents like us to make sure these schools improve." Yet, despite her resolve, Yvonne found the transition process, in her own word "excruciating".

When her primary class went to visit Tanya was terrified because it was chaos. Not just that, the kids were pretty crazy, they weren't in the classrooms, the ones in the classrooms weren't getting on with their work and the teachers didn't seem to have much control, it was just chaos. I rang up the head and said I came today and do you know, we want to send our daughter to this school, we really want to support this school because [of] everything we believe about putting into your community and not taking from it, this encompasses everything we believe, we want to come, and we will help, and I said, look, today was a complete disaster and my daughter already asked not to go to school and had to listen to her friends saying oh, why are your parents sending you to that crap school, my mum would never let me go. And we are getting flak from them, and then we are getting her here and it was a disaster. So it was just excruciating … I felt sick nearly all the time. (Yvonne, white, middle-class mother)

For Yvonne, her investment in doing what was best for society rather than just her own children was producing considerable anxiety, not only in relation to her daughter's fraught experience of the local comprehensive but also in terms of her own self-perception as a mother who, in sending her child to what is perceived to be 'a bad school', may herself be seen to be 'a bad mother'. We can see very clearly the conflict and tension between being a good citizen and a good parent:

She went on the first day and literally I was not sleeping at night and everything, I was really worried. And I am not a worrier, I am really not, but the first day she went, I took her there, and me and David both took her and she went up the stairs to the door to the assembly hall and she didn't know anybody and she walked off, and her face, I will never forget her face, and she went "bye mum" and then I went and worried all day, all day I was looking at my watch and worrying. (Yvonne, white, middle-class mother)

Concerns about getting it right and doing the right thing are engendered and reinforced by social networks. When, in Yvonne's words, those in your wider social networks "peel off for the private and selective state sector", parents like Yvonne are left with a sense of abandonment, but also intense anxiety and guilt. There is no reassurance of community. Instead we can see very powerfully the psychic costs of principled choice in this context. The strategies Yvonne develops for defending against the obviously painful feelings that anxiety provokes are institutional as well as personal. Like over 50% of our middle-class sample, she becomes involved in the school and, at the time of the interview, was chair of the governing body. Yet, as she told me, her belief that this would allay her fears proved to be unfounded. As she confided, "if anything I am more anxious – before, I worried about not knowing enough about what was going on, now I worry because I know far too much".

Conclusion

Within the public arenas of the social and, more specifically, the educational world, there is a growing emphasis on competition, instrumentalism and 'being the best', while the demonisation of the working-class, and in particular the white working-class, within official, media and public discourses, has increased since the mid-1960s. All these developments have impacted powerfully on what it feels to be upper, middle and working class, as well as the internal dynamics through which individuals create and justify boundary constructions in relation to class. I have not drawn on a case study from the upper classes because, although there was often a lot of emotion in interviews with the upper-class families, the emotions expressed were primarily those of contempt, superiority or disdain rather than anxiety, ambivalence, guilt or fear. Rather, along with the working classes, it was a section of the middle classes, those who sent their children to state comprehensives, and in particular those who had grown up working class, whose interviews were saturated with emotion. Stallybrass and White describe the middle-class as:

> a class which, whilst indeed progressive in its best political aspirations, had encoded in its manners, morals and imaginative writings, in its body, bearing and taste, a subliminal elitism which was constitutive of its historical being. Whatever the radical nature of its 'universal' democratic demand, it had engraved in its subjective identity all the marks by which it felt itself to be a different, distinctive and superior class.[17]

However, unlike in the case of the upper classes, this subliminal elitism was often undercut by an insecurity and fragility that was expressed through emotions of anxiety and ambivalence. Although this book is about the working classes and education, what I hope to have conveyed through including the examples of Max, Camilla and Yvonne is the damage that an unfair and hyper-competitive educational system inflicts on all children, and the emotional fall-out for them and their families across social class differences.

In the next chapter I move on to discuss the continuities and transformations over the recent history of the working-class relationship to education, exploring what has changed and what has remained the same since Jackson and Marsden wrote their ground-breaking book. I then attempt to draw out possibilities for improving working-class educational experiences, but with a key proviso that it is not just policies that will need to change, but deeply engrained social values, as well as widespread attitudes to inequality, welfare and difference.

EIGHT

Conclusion

Continuities and transformations: what has changed since Jackson and Marsden and what has remained the same?

The continuities

This book has been an attempt to follow in the path of Jackson and Marsden's ground-breaking book on education and the working classes. Although their book is commonly seen to focus on the successful working classes, a haunting presence in the book are those working classes who were not educationally successful, those in the lower sets, technical schools and secondary moderns – the vast majority of the working classes, then as now, who are left to fail. I hope I have demonstrated that a further theme throughout their book was the damage done to the working classes, even those who were seen to be educationally successful. While the differences and changes between Jackson and Marsden's 1950s and 1960s and today are what immediately strike the reader, this first section of the conclusion also focuses on a number of arresting continuities. In particular, it is argued that, despite myriad educational policy changes, the English educational system is still one that educates individuals according to their class background. It remains a segregated system where different social classes are largely educated apart rather than together. Also, the ways in which social mobility operates to dislocate the educationally successful working classes from their communities of origin is just as pervasive as it was at the time when Jackson and Marsden were writing.

The most troubling continuity is that most working-class children and young people experience education as failure. I have tried to explain why this is still the case in the face of so many policy initiatives to improve working-class educational attainment. I have argued that in place of 'the usual suspects', namely either working-class culture or the 'failing' schools that invariably have predominantly working-class and BME intakes, we need to focus on the operations of power within education. This involves looking at relational aspects of educational achievement and examining the actions and attitudes of the middle and upper classes as well as those of the working classes. It also requires a historical, contextualised perspective that recognises over a century of class domination within state schooling, and the symbolic power of the private sector that continues to be held up as embodying all that is best in English education.

In 1995 a black, working-class lone mother whom I interviewed evocatively summed up the state of education as she saw it. She could have been talking about the late 2010s.

> *Starting with the assumption we are not a racist society and now that we are a classless society, the problems are being swept away so no one has to deal with these issues. People are no longer privileged because they are white, they are no longer privileged because they are middle class. It's scary. It's frightening. What also frightens me is that after 100 years of state education we are still not sure why we are educating the working classes. There are no jobs for them and the government doesn't want thinkers. They just need people to be controlled in the classroom, to keep them busy, churning out a whole lot of facts, keep them so busy they don't have time to analyse, no time to question the way things are. Schools are becoming like businesses and a business is nothing to do with all those things we have been talking about. It is about efficiency, money, productivity and so things like human rights and social justice just go right off the agenda.* (Cassie, black, working-class mother)

As Cassie eloquently points out, the underlying purpose of English education is neither to realise the potential of all children nor to provide equal opportunities for academic success. Rather, it is still about the control and containment Adam Smith wrote about more than two centuries ago. But, as Cassie also indicates, one significant difference is the culture of business, competition and privatisation that has pervaded the English educational system and is marginalising already fragile commitments to social justice and fairness. In the years since that interview all these trends that Cassie describes have intensified. Schools are now run like businesses, there is a growing preoccupation with finance, productivity and efficiency, we have a labour market without valued working-class jobs and a curriculum that gets in the way of thinking, rather than encouraging it.

A further key continuity with the past is that, despite a very different educational landscape, with a very different range of schools, and the establishment of the National Curriculum, which supposedly offers the same curriculum to all children regardless of their class background, educational success is still restricted to a few. And those few are predominantly upper and middle class. As I was writing this book the Sutton Trust published a report: *Global Gaps: Comparing socio-economic gaps in the performance of highly able UK pupils internationally.*[1] Looking at the 2015 PISA (Programme for International Student Assessment) results, it found that the gap between the middle and working class within what it calls 'the top 10% most able students' in each class grouping was 33 months in science and maths and 32 months in reading. This rose to a three-year gap in reading between high-achieving working-class girls and their high-achieving middle-class peers. Even 'highly able' working-class students in England are falling far behind middle-class students, despite a wide range of recent policies focused specifically on them.

One explanation is that our educational system has never moved from an elite to a mass system. Elitism remains at its core. We still have to deal with the dominance of the private school system and its graduates at our elite universities, at the top of all our professions, but also symbolically as representing what is 'the best' in English society. This is largely a consequence of having an educational system that still operates as a form of social apartheid. In *Education and the Working Class* Dennis Marsden and Brian Jackson drew on their own experiences to problematise the apartheid that operated in the 1960s tripartite system. As their book powerfully illustrated, this system produced rifts and divisions between educationally successful working-class individuals and the families and neighbourhoods they came from. As Sol Gamsu argues:

> For the grammar schools involved, and post-war society more widely, working class 11-plus successes provided a sort of 'social alibi' which allowed the justification of a system of education that still overwhelmingly benefitted the middle and upper classes, at secondary and university level.[2]

He concludes that 'the class elitism inherent in the logic of "raising up" a gifted few through the 11-plus was never seriously challenged and has returned with a vengeance in the widening participation discourse at elite universities'. Now that we have moved to a mass system of higher education, the logic of 'the educational ladder' and the insidious ideological alibi that it provides has simply moved upwards. Instead of the 11-plus operating as a mechanism of social selection it is our elite universities that have taken over this role. Elitist processes masquerading as meritocracy are just as evident in the English educational system as they were 60 years ago in the 1950s; but the primary engines of this pseudo meritocracy are no longer the grammar schools but the elite universities.

But those who are socially mobile have to cope with the pernicious as well as the positive effects of social mobility, just as Jackson and Marsden's Oxbridge boys did 50 years ago. Now we have growing medical evidence that poverty in early childhood, and dealing with often hostile and unfamiliar environments such as the middle-class school and university, literally gets under the skin and damages socially mobile individuals physically as well as psychologically. The social challenges that are part and parcel of social mobility become biologically embedded, resulting in stress, inflammation and premature ageing,[3] and this is as true today as it was when *Education and the Working Class* was written.

While the upper classes and most of the middle classes have been insulated from austerity and its consequences, most of the working classes are struggling. Austerity is mainly for those who are already poor. Their children are also increasingly experiencing 'austerity education'. As Saltman, writing about American education in the 21st century, argues:

> Austerity education is not only about a turn to repressive control of youth in the interests of amassing profits for the rich, creating a docile and disciplined workforce as the conditions of work and life are worsened for the majority of citizens. It is also about the rightist project of capturing public space such as schools to actively produce politically illiterate, socially uncritical, and un-self critical subject positions for youth to occupy.[4]

Such right-wing projects were powerfully resonant of the 19th-century upper- and middle-class mission to control and pacify the working classes rather than to educate them. Our new austerity world of Brexit and Donald Trump may feel unsettling and unfamiliar, but austerity education is a return to the past. Just as was the case in the 19th century, we are educating the working classes to be subservient and compliant, cramming them with facts, and then continually testing their recall. Such teaching to the test means that political awareness, critical thinking and problem solving have all been neglected. One of the major forms of the miseducation of the working classes is that we are still educating them for the 19th century in the 21st.

... and the changes

Differences in class experiences in education are even more complex and multifaceted than when Jackson and Marsden were writing. Frequently used indicators of social class, namely occupation and educational qualifications, tell only half of the story of class experiences in education. They are more completely understood in terms of confidence and entitlement in relation to education, the amount of knowledge and information about the school system that families have, the social networks that families have access to, wealth or the lack of it; but also whether you come to school with a family history of educational success and recognition, or with a sense that education is not something you and your family are good at. What I hope the book has shown is that, just as success breeds success, failure turns into more failure. Getting low grades in your SATs, low marks in a test, being placed in a bottom set or simply receiving little attention and, in particular, little praise all conspire to make the working-class experience of education one in which success is, at best, tenuous and failure often feels inevitable. Once this would have been seen as a problem that the whole of English society, and especially those who govern it, needed to address. Now, increasingly, it is viewed as the fault of the working-class individual. This raises serious issues around independence and dependence, autonomy and insufficiency in which working-classness is viewed as a matter of internal traits rather than economic position, and class inequalities become just the natural order of things because working-class individuals who fail to be socially mobile are seen to lack the right qualities rather than sufficient resources. An irony is that while the working classes are judged harshly for remaining in the same social and economic space they grew up in, the middle and upper classes are held up as positive role models for similarly staying fixed in space. And hardly anyone points out that the unfair levels of economic, cultural and social resources that enable the latter groups to stay in place are also fixing the working classes in place. The growth of competitive individualism, the erosion of secure jobs in the labour market and escalating housing prices have all had detrimental effects on working-class families. And conditions for the working classes are set to deteriorate even further. The Resolution Foundation argues that the period from 2015/16 to 2020/21 is on course to be the worst on record for income growth in the bottom half of the UK population.[5] At the same time, the report predicts the biggest rise in inequality since the 1980s, with inequality reaching record highs by 2020/21.

When I was growing up there was a sense of optimism and hope for the future. Parents like my own, who had left school early, felt that they could make a positive contribution to their children's future by working hard and enabling them to stay on at school. They believed that they could contribute to their children having a better life than they had. This is no longer the case for a majority of working-class parents. They can no longer envisage their own children having access to assets such as homeownership that they once took for granted. Many of them confront the prospect that their children may well be worse off than they are, denied a secure job, unable to afford to buy their own home and, if they do make it to university, saddled with debts that could take a lifetime to pay off. In no small part these fears and anxieties, and the growing resentment and anger they have given rise to, lie at the root of phenomena like the referendum vote to leave the European Union.

A further thing that has changed since the 1960s is the preoccupation with economic efficiency as an educational goal. In 21st-century England arguments that favour redistribution and public ownership have been over-shadowed by political perspectives that accept growing social inequalities and support the free market and privatisation. This has led to the emphasis on performativity within education, the downgrading of education as a right in itself and an increasing preoccupation with education as a means to economic ends. Jackson and Marsden do not mention education in relation to the economy, but from the late 1970s any concern with social justice in education has been increasingly eclipsed by the focus on economic efficiency and the role that the educational system is seen as having to play in improving economic productivity and growth. This harnessing of education to the needs of the wider economy has both a narrowing and a diminishing impact, limiting the possibilities and scope of education in terms of social justice and fairness. It also has a powerful effect on both the organisation and ethos of education. While social justice requires bringing students together to collaborate across social differences, economic efficiency emphasises differentiation through competition and the growing tolerance of profit making in the public sector. This has implications for what is acceptable within education.

Jackson and Marsden would be shocked to discover the extent to which education in the 21st century has become a money-making enterprise. So, for example, teacher supply agencies were paid £733 million in 2014, but by 2016 this had risen to £1.26 billion a year, a 38% increase in three years. Teacher supply agencies are making huge profits from state funding for schools, yet an NUT survey showed that in 2015 many supply teachers were paid less by agencies than they were in 2012, and were not entitled to sick pay, maternity pay or teachers' pensions. One teaching agency made a profit in 2014 of £15.4 million on a turnover of £63.7million.[6]

A further cause of change since Jackson and Marsden were writing in the 1960s is that the working classes as a clearly identifiable group have shrunk from 60% to around 40% of the English population. This has left them more exposed to pathologisation and feelings of failure because, as Evans and Tilley argue, becoming a smaller group at the bottom of the class hierarchy has made it increasingly difficult to avoid unfavourable comparisons.[7] In the 1950s and 1960s, when they were the largest class grouping in society, such negative stereotyping was less likely to occur, although both Jackson and Marsden's and my own experiences show that it still did. As Evans and Tilley conclude, working-class people both accepted their situation and were less likely to be judged when they constituted the majority. However, the shrinking of traditional working-class jobs has not been matched by a corresponding expansion of professional and managerial jobs in the labour market. Unlike the period when Jackson and Marsden were writing, when there was a rapid expansion of professional and managerial posts in the economy, the Labour Force Survey found that between 1997 and 2014 the annual increase in the number of professional and managerial jobs was just over 80,000 a year. Rather, between 1997 and 2016 the greatest expansion in the labour market has been in service sector jobs, which increased from 63.2% to a huge 83.5% of the total proportion of jobs.[8] This is a group that Evans and Tilley would categorise as 'routine non-manual', and therefore middle class. But for a majority of service sector workers like my sister, and Rosie and Assiz whom I mentioned in Chapter Five, poor working conditions, levels of pay, job insecurity and low status would mean that they have more in common with the working-class rather than the middle classes.

Today, to be working class is to be a loser in a more unequal and socially differentiated society than the England that Jackson and Marsden were writing about. This has the dire educational consequences that I have chronicled in earlier chapters. In the next section I focus on what we can do to change continuing educational inequalities.

Why do the working classes fare so much worse in education than the upper and middle classes? What can we do about it?

In this second part of the conclusion I update and build on insights from earlier work[9] in order to introduce readers to understandings that they can draw on to actively work against the injuries of class they confront in their everyday lives, in institutional practices and in educational policy. Jackson and Marsden closed their book with the following words:

> It is now clearer to see that the old purpose of education – the training of a ruling elite – has not collapsed under the new purpose – the training of enough people to man our technological society. More and more the two are allies, putting the same people in the same places at the same price ... but it need not be so.[10]

As a grammar school pupil I was constantly told by the other girls that I had 'a chip on my shoulder'. At the time it felt like yet another thing I was getting wrong, a measure of my failure to fit in and comply. But, in retrospect, it was a powerful source of working-class strength, a sense of righteous indignation at the unfairness of working-class life in an unequal society. I hope this book has conveyed a sense of how unfair the educational world is for those who occupy an inferior, devalued position in the educational field. Working-class relationships to education have always been deeply problematic and emotionally charged, inscribing academic failure rather than success.

Currently, in the wake of Brexit, a lot of the working classes are identified as having 'a chip on the shoulder', angry at being left behind and left out of economic and social advances that have primarily advantaged the rich. But they have always been left behind in English education, where social mobility, a mechanism that depletes rather than enriches the working classes, has been the main strategy for addressing class inequalities in education. The English educational system has always helped the middle and upper classes to feel at ease in the world, and confident about their options and opinions, while it instils in the working classes a sense of their limitations and the feeling of having few options. If you wanted to design an educational system that discouraged and demoralised working-class children it would be hard to come up with anything as effective as the English one. Jessica Gerrard has argued:

> The collective naming of shared experiences of inequality and oppression is central to developing grounds for challenging social inequality, whether this be on the basis of class, race, gender, or something else.[11]

And the working classes have always been oppressed within English state education. As Terry Eagleton wrote in 1991:

> Someone is being oppressed not simply if they drag out a wretched existence, but if certain creative capacities they could feasibly realise are being actively thwarted by the unjust interest of others.[12]

The working classes have routinely been set up to fail throughout the entire history of English state schooling so that their more privileged class 'others' can succeed. Their potential is, and has been, 'thwarted by the unjust interest of others'. From Steve McQueen's many beautiful people who 'didn't achieve what they could achieve because no one believed in them, or gave them a chance, or invested any time in them', to Josie and her sons, the normative working-class educational experience is one of neglect, unrealised potential, an unfair allocation of resources and exploitation and oppression. As John Smyth and Robin Simmons outline in the introduction to their edited book *Education and Working Class Youth*,[13] a plethora of spectacular educational irrelevancies such as standards, testing regimes, raising attainment and achievement levels, league tables, school choice, academies and charter schools, performativities and managerialism, image and impression management, academic/vocational streaming, punitive naming and shaming strategies and the rhetoric of school improvement and school effectiveness have obscured the crucial importance of social class to educational success.

The working classes have never had a fair chance in education. They did not have a fair chance when Jackson and Marsden were writing, and they definitely do not have one in a 21st-century England that is scarred by growing inequalities. The rhetoric of equality, fairness and freedom in education has intensified since the beginning of this century, but it has done so against a back-drop of ever-increasing inequalities, the entrenchment of neoliberalism and class domination. It is predominantly babble, signifying little, and certainly nothing that will make any contribution to a fairer, more equal educational system. In the aspirational society that England has become, there is intense competition for 'fair chances' as upper- and middle-class parents strategise and invest in order for their children to have a better 'fair chance' than other people's children. This is about transmitting and solidifying advantage, and works against rather than promoting social justice. Within the field of education the working classes have increasingly become what is to be avoided, and as economic austerity has grown and the poor have become poorer, working-class exclusions within education have both deepened and extended. So the key question to ask is: how are we going to change the English educational system so that it is both fairer and better equipped to prepare all its students for the many complex challenges of the 21st century?

If we sum up the main reasons why the working classes continue to fail educationally, a number of influences stand out.

- *The importance of history:* we cannot make sense of contemporary working-class underachievement without investigating its historical roots, and recognising that the original purpose of providing state education for all was to keep working-class political and economic ambitions in check, not to realise them. From the outset, the upper and middle classes wanted a docile, obedient working class, not one that aspired to equal recognition, respect and rewards.

- *The relational nature of class:* working-class underachievement is about not just the attitudes and behavior of the working classes but also the attitudes and behaviour of the upper and middle classes and the relationships between all three classes – 'no class is an island'. Relatedly, the private school system is still the ideal – the paragon against which state education continues to be evaluated and measured. As long as this remains the case there is little hope of social justice for the working classes in English education.

- *The importance of wider social and economic conditions:* schools reflect the wider society's attitudes and values and, crucially, its distribution of resources, rather than being able to compensate for them. We are at a very low point in relation to working-class power and rights within the wider economy, both in relation to the share of economic gains and because of the receding protective role of the state in welfare capitalism. An effective policy for tackling working-class underachievement would have to redress current economic and social inequalities.

- *The shifting of educational responsibilities onto families:* the English state and its governing elite have increasingly expected families to take on educational responsibilities that in the 1960s and 1970s would have been viewed as the remit of the state and its educational system. The commonplace assumption is now that parents will subsidise and augment the work of schools through educational work in the home, private tuition, paying for enrichment activities and, increasingly, giving financial donations to schools.[14] The same reliance on family resources is growing in the higher education sector, with the state assuming that families will contribute as student loans increasingly fail to cover expenses.[15] But, as earlier chapters have shown, working-class families, as well as growing numbers of financially hard-pressed middle-class families, lack the resources to provide the expected support.

As Antonucci concludes, such 'reliance on family resources has a direct effect on the reproduction of inequality'.[16]

So what will improve the educational experiences of working-class children?

Educational policies do have an impact, particularly on working-class experiences of education. Current policies that emphasise diversity, choice, testing and streaming have increased segregation and polarisation, both between schools and within them. Yet both the OECD[17] and PISA have come to the conclusion that securing diversity within schools rather than between schools is the best route for any government to take if it wishes to enable all young people to reach high standards of achievement. As the evidence I have presented in this book demonstrates, government policies for school provision that encourage parents to choose from a diverse range of schools lead to social class segregation. But we also need to tackle inter-school segregation, as social distance between social classes has grown in schools, mirroring the growing social distance in wider society.

English education needs to break free from the class constraints that have restricted its vision and practices over the centuries. A new, progressive agenda does not have to be idealistically utopian – it can be grounded in and grow out of a long-standing evidence base[18] that shows, for example, that setting and streaming and raising aspirations do not work, and collaborative learning does.

Research studies dating back over 30 years, to the early 1980s, have consistently shown that setting and streaming benefits high-attaining students but is detrimental to the learning of middle- and lower-attaining students.[19] It benefits the academic progress of the few, at the expense of the many. But the case against setting and streaming does not just have historical validity, it also has geographical credentials. Lucy Crehan, in her book *Cleverlands*, found that both separating students into different schools and separating them into different sets and streams at an early age leads to 'inequalities in a system; a larger spread of results, with those results being more heavily determined by parental background and immigration status'.[20] Four out of the five high-performing countries that she visited taught children in mixed-ability classes until they were aged 15 or 16. But this is not simply an issue of academic performance. Research, including my own, has exposed the ways in which setting and streaming seriously undermines the confidence and well-being of those in the lower sets. Research on ability groups also shows high levels of misplacement, in which set allocation is often more closely related to social class background than to ability level.[21] It is an inefficient educational strategy in terms of raising overall educational attainment and it damages the many working-class and the few middle-class children who end up in bottom sets. Moreover, the inequalities intrinsic to practices of setting and streaming are compounded by organisational factors. Higher-attainment sets are more likely to have experienced and highly qualified teachers, whereas lower sets experience more changes of teacher and are less likely to be taught by a specialist in the subject.

I have already written in Chapter Two about the fallacy that the working classes lack aspirations. In its summary of the effect of interventions to raise aspirations, the Education Endowment Foundation (EEF) found that, overall, they appeared to have little to no positive impact on educational attainment. As the research shows, this is partly because young people and their parents already have high aspirations.[22] But high aspirations do not automatically translate into high attainment, especially for the many working-class students who lack the resources for educational success.

In contrast, research over a 40-year period demonstrates that the impact of collaborative approaches to learning is consistently positive and enhances attainment.[23] This extensive body of research also indicates that approaches that promote talk and interaction between learners tend to result in the most gains. This may seem to challenge common-sense understandings of what promotes educational attainment, because educational policy since the 1980s has predominantly been about increasing competition in schools. Yet, approaches that are totally counter to the individualised, competitive pedagogies that are endemic in English schools produce significant gains in attainment for all students. The EEF concludes that cooperation is considerably more effective than interpersonal competition and individualistic efforts, and has the added bonus of enhancing attitudes to learning as well as achievement. In view of this extensive evidence base that reveals the failure of common policies and practices within English education to improve attainment, and the success of policies and practices that have been abandoned as too child centred, the key question that needs to be asked is why English education has never embraced approaches that work and adopts those that don't.

In fact, despite the polemics about child-centred education and progressive learning practices, English education has never been particularly progressive in its teaching methods. A number of high-performing countries like Canada and Finland have always been much more progressive. But even countries that are seen to have more traditional practices turn out to be more progressive than England. While 37% of English secondary maths teachers believe that it is most important to learn by heart, only 25% of China/Shanghai teachers do. In England 35% of students say they are given an opportunity to express an opinion in their maths lesson, while for Shanghai students the figure is 47%.[24] In an ironic reversal, English private schools are now often more progressive in their teaching practices than English state schools. As Laura McInerney found, state school pupils reported more traditional teaching, while private school students reported higher rates of being asked to express opinions in class, completing group work and having their teacher relate their learning to their lives.[25]

One policy that, according to the EEF, lacks a decisive evidence base is the promotion of parental choice in education. But there are a number of research studies that show that the working classes are often left with the choices the middle classes don't want to make.[26] Choice for the working classes involves either a process of finding out what you can't have, what is not open for negotiation and then looking at the few options left, or a process of self-exclusion that originates in a deeply engrained sense that selective and high-status schools are not places for 'people like us'. This focus on choice has entrenched processes of segregation and polarisation in English schools. Parental choice policies mean that now only half of English secondary school pupils attending a state school actually go to their nearest school,[27] whereas research shows that if more students attended their nearest school, levels of social class segregation would be lower.[28]

Diversifying the types of school has exacerbated these processes further. Introducing a range of different types of school, supposedly in the interests of giving parents more choice, has been shown to increase differences between schools and lead to more social class polarisation. The academies and free schools policies are too recent to have any significant evidence base as to their impact on class inequalities in education, but the early signs that I refer to in Chapter Two do not look good. Early evidence from a research study covering 79 schools found that at primary school level free schools are enrolling children with above-average ability, namely recruiting a disproportionate number of middle-class children.[29]

Similarly, the preoccupation with assessment and testing has no reliable evidence base in terms of raising educational attainment, while I have shown throughout the book that it has a demonstrable negative impact on working-class children's self-worth and self-esteem as learners. Rather, recent findings reveal that the gap between FSM and other children has increased, for example from 8 percentage points in Maths at Key Stage 1 in 2015 to 18 percentage points in 2016.[30]

I have talked about the benefits of cooperation within classrooms; equally important is cooperation between schools. The growing schools cooperative movement rejects what it sees as a developing semi-privatised education system, with academy brands competing in a market structure that is underpinned by the values of corporate business.[31] It contrasts what it sees as the democracy of the cooperative movement with the competitive, individualised ethos of the English educational market-place. Currently, there are around 800 cooperative schools in England. While the first were single schools, most now comprise clusters of schools across a geographical area, with the structure providing a framework for sharing expertise and resources. This growing cooperative movement prioritises collaboration as opposed to the competition that defines much of the schooling market, and all the schools joining are encouraged to embrace a cooperative ethos underpinned by the values of self-help, self-responsibility, democracy, equality and solidarity. This slowly growing community of schools provides a much-needed antidote to the growing commodification and fragmentation of English education.

If we were to implement all the policy changes I am suggesting, schools would be more enhancing and positive places for all children across social class. But we also need a sea-change in the ways we think about, value, recognise and respect the working classes. This would definitely not be about building on existing best practice or aspects of what has gone before, because the English educational system has never got this right. I am arguing for something that has never seriously been attempted, let alone achieved, within English education, namely, social justice for the working classes. We need an educational system that accords respect to the working classes and attributes positive value to working-classness. In *Pedagogy of the Oppressed* Paolo Freire wrote of education having one of two functions within society: either as an instrument of conformity, socialising younger generations into the logic of the existing system – in the present case, into compliance with neoliberal capitalism; or else to operate as 'the practice of freedom', enabling children and young people to engage critically and reflexively with the society they are part of, and to learn how to participate in transforming it for the better.[32]

This would necessitate very different relationships between schools and working-class communities; relationships that reconnect education to democracy and schools to their communities. There are lots of guidelines from the past. America's John Dewey wrote *My Pedagogic Creed* 120 years ago,[33] but it remains a testament to democratic participatory education that emphasised the importance of viewing children as an end in themselves, and their interests and experiences as vital starting points for teaching and learning. He believed that schools should value and reflect the learning that goes on in the home and the locality, arguing that 'the school must represent present life – life as real and vital to the child as that which he carries on in the home, in the neighborhood, or on the playground'.[34] This would require an educative relationship between schools and working-class communities, one that works in both directions.

More recently, bell hooks, the American feminist, has written about the idea of education as a collective practice of thinking together and making sense of the world. She asserts that 'to teach in a manner that respects and cares for the souls of our students is essential if we are to provide the necessary conditions where learning can most deeply and intimately begin'.[35] Her educational model is based on intense personal relationships between students and teachers that aim to empower students to recognise their authority as legitimate knowers in the world. She claims that the most fertile ground for progressive social change is teaching critical skills to individuals, rather than focusing on large-scale progressive social and political action. What is needed is an 'engaged pedagogy' that focuses on the self-actualisation, empowerment and well-being of students. For hooks, the most engaged and rewarding critical thinking is done with other people. It relies on collaborative efforts, like reasoning through problems in groups, to ensure that we are respectful and responsible to the interests and experiences of others as they relate to the issue at hand, and to ensure that as many potentially competing assumptions and perspectives as possible can be raised to maintain the integrity of the critical thinking process.[36] The practical wisdom[37] that grows out of critical thinking is both grounded in and generates empathy, care, compassion and understanding of both the self and others.

The changes I propose will benefit all children and young people, not just those who are working class. As I have argued throughout this book, while the working classes are those who suffer the most, our current unjust educational system damages all children. As Raoul Martinez argues:

> The combination of dress codes, rigid syllabi, set lessons, constant examination, hours of passive listening and an absence of internal democracy mean that schooldays are typically characterised by tight control. Study is geared to exams, which grants great power to those who set them and little autonomy to those who take them. The sheer quantity of disconnected units of information leaves students struggling to keep up. Careful attention to a syllabus is rewarded over careful attention to one's curiosity. Regurgitation of facts is rewarded over originality,

passionate engagement or independent thought. These arrangements prepare students for a society in which they have little say over the decisions that affect their lives.[38]

Jackson and Marsden were saddened by many of the experiences of the working-class whom they interviewed for their study of *Education and the Working Class*. Their passionate concern and compassion would be shot through with a sense of righteous indignation if they were researching working-class education today. There is so much to do and, on the surface, so little will to do it. That needs to change. I hope that this book will be one of many efforts to open up possibilities for an educational system that enhances the well-being, critical awareness and intellectual development of all children. But most of all we need social justice in education for the working classes.

A qualification

After writing the last section on how to improve the existing educational system, and beyond that achieve socially just education for the working classes, I am left, as with past attempts, with a sense of being simplistic, superficial, even hypocritical. For example, as Francis et al argue, research findings on the benefits of mixed-ability teaching appear to have had little impact on policy and practice in English education, where setting continues to predominate in practice and to be actively promoted by policy makers, in spite of the research evidence.[39] As they point out, this can be explained by the power that practices of academic segregation hold as symbols of academic 'standards'. They are seen as endorsing 'natural' hierarchies that appeal powerfully to contemporary middle-class desire and aspirations.

We are living in an England where most people espouse 'a resigned reluctant individualism',[40] in a country where feelings of fellow connection, empathy and understanding across social differences and an inclusive sense of community are no longer characteristic of the working classes and have never been part of normative middle- and upper-class identity. The response of the political elite to an austerity created by our economic elite is to penalise the poorest and impose an austerity education on their children. The convention in a book like this is to set out the problems and then to offer solutions. But our current situation defies any formulaic approach. What is needed is a sea-change in hearts and minds, not just better policy in education. As Grasso et al argue, young people coming of age under sustained periods of Conservative government have absorbed the right-wing values of those governments, offsetting the tendency towards social liberalism that is normally characteristic of the young.[41] They conclude that those coming of age during Margaret Thatcher and John Major's time in office are particularly conservative, and deserving of the label 'Thatcher's children'. But, more concerning, they found evidence of her 'grandchildren' in the generation born between 1979 and 1990. These, who grew up to become 'Blair's babies', are even more right wing and authoritarian in their attitudes to redistribution and welfare. A recent international survey conducted in 20 countries found that UK young people were among the least likely to think that it is important to contribute to wider society beyond themselves and their family and friends.[42] As Grasso et al conclude, as a generation they are more likely than their parents and grandparents to agree that income inequality is too small and state benefits are too high.[43] Such findings are borne out in the following conclusion by Peter Taylor-Gooby:

> The mass public appears less sympathetic to the poor, less generous to the unemployed and less concerned about inequalities. These patterns are reflected in newspaper discourse and the programmes of political parties. The upshot is that the pressures on the poor and on those parts of the welfare state that provide for them are increasingly severe, while there is little support for policies to address these issues.[44]

As Taylor-Gooby comments in relation to the British focus groups he interviewed in 2015, 'no one mentioned a collective solution to the problems they identified at all. It was as if institutions like trade unions and local government had never existed'.[45] There are, however, growing glimmers of hope. For the first time since the financial crash of 2007/08, more people (48%) want taxation increased to allow greater spending, than want tax and spending levels to stay as they are (44%).[46] The fight for social justice in education is also a fight to encourage increasing support for redistribution and challenge the more right-wing, individualistic and authoritarian attitudes that have been common across all sectors and generations of English society over the past decade. While I am passionately in favour of redistribution and a well-resourced, inclusive welfare system, it would also be arrogant to think I escape the reluctant, resigned individualism any more than the always middle-class individual does. I often despair. But I have an anger about the unequal way things are that is still as strong as it was 50 years ago. I will continue to struggle against social class injustices, and this book is part of my struggle.

Epilogue: thinking through class

In *Education and the Working Class* Jackson and Marsden included an appendix that was nominally about further research, but in essence was the two authors thinking through class in education. I would like to end with a personal reflection on thinking through class that attempts to capture some of their 'visionary gleam'[1] and transpose it to the 21st century.

Keeping people stuck in segregated areas, in demeaning jobs without sufficient income and consigned to a life with little hope and prospect that things will get better can breed racism, bigotry, ignorance and narrow-mindedness. Such attitudes have nothing to do with the intrinsic qualities of the people themselves and everything to do with the consequences of their circumstances. So the important thing to do is to change those circumstances – in the workplace, in the local area, and also in schools and classrooms. And we should not expect people to transform their own lives when they haven't been given the resources to make that possible. That's unfair, it is expecting miracles when miracles very, very rarely happen.

But I see the direction my own life has taken as a kind of miracle. Pierre Bourdieu, who had a similar miraculous trajectory, said in an interview in 1992:

> My main problem is to try to understand what happened to me. My trajectory may be described as miraculous, I suppose – an ascension to a place where I don't belong. And so to be able to live in a world that is not mine I must try to understand both things: what it means to have an academic mind – how such is created – and at the same time what was lost in

acquiring it. For that reason, even if my work – my full work – is a sort of auto-biography, it is a work for people who have the same sort of trajectory, and the same need to understand.[2]

I have a similar need to understand, and this book has been part of a process of thinking through class – both my own changed class position and also relationships between the class I am now ambivalently part of and the class I have left. That leaving was at times traumatic and laden with grief, even as it was being desperately yearned for. Perhaps the most powerful lesson I learnt from my childhood is that no child should be left in poverty, written off educationally and viewed as having a lower value than other children whose main difference is that they have had the good fortune to be born into more privileged families. Many of those of us who grew up as FSM children, left to line up and have our names ticked off after all the normal children had been registered, want a more equal world in which there is no longer a need for FSM, or for that matter food banks or the myriad other things that are about ritual humiliation because you and your family have the audacity to be poor. But we often find that we too are ensnared in dominant representations of the working classes, and struggle to find ways of 'speaking against poverty and indignity without speaking against who we are, what we are like, and where we are from'.[3] This book is an attempt, one of many I have made, to talk back, to work with working-class people's words rather than to work on them. Being an academic makes such speaking out harder, as it involves stepping back, aiming for objectivity. This book, then, is trying to cut across the grain of what I have become professionally. It is in many ways a very personal perspective on education and the working classes. It has used very little of Pierre Bourdieu's theory (unlike most of my academic work) and has drawn as much on my experiences as a working-class child, and later as a primary school teacher of 20 years' standing, as it has done on my academic experience.

As Annette Kuhn reflects:

Perhaps for those of us who learned silence through shame, the hardest thing of all is to find a voice; not

the voice of the monstrous, singular ego, but one that,
summoning the resources of the place we come from,
can speak with eloquence of, and for, that place.[4]

This book is my attempt to speak with eloquence of, and for,
that place.

Notes

Introduction

[1] Jackson and Marsden, 1966.
[2] Bradley, 1996, p 19.
[3] Hanley, 2016.
[4] Lawler, 2014, p 703.
[5] Jones, 2011.
[6] Jackson and Marsden, 1966, p 180.
[7] Jones, 2016.
[8] Heath et al, 2013.
[9] British Social Attitudes Survey, 2016.
[10] Ibid, p 6.
[11] Jackson and Marsden, 1966, p 214.

Chapter One

[1] Bernstein, 1970.
[2] Jackson and Marsden, 1966, p 246.
[3] Todd, 2014.
[4] Steedman, 1986, p 122.
[5] Kynaston, 2009.
[6] House of Commons Education Committee, 2014.
[7] Ryan, 2016.
[8] Walker, 2016.
[9] JRF, 2016.
[10] Ibid, p 142.
[11] Trading Economics, 2016.
[12] Heath, 2016.
[13] Ibid.
[14] Heath, 2016, p 11.
[15] Mani et al, 2013.
[16] Robinson and Fielding, 2007.
[17] Lareau, 2003.
[18] Coren, 2016.
[19] Beyond the Fringe, 1964 (Acting Edition).
[20] Elliott, 2016.

21 Clarke and D'Arcy, 2016.
22 HMRC, 2016.
23 Resolution Foundation, 2012, p 16.
24 Jacques, 2016.
25 House of Commons Business, Innovation and Skills Committee, 2016a, p 3.
26 Ibid, p 9.
27 Ibid, p 12.
28 Ibid, p 26.
29 House of Commons Business, Innovation and Skills Committee, 2016b.
30 Foster, 2015, p 9.
31 Jones, 2011; Tyler, 2008; 2010.
32 Bennett, 2012.
33 Jensen, 2013.
34 Bennett, 2012, p 147.
35 House of Commons Education Committee, 2014, p 27.
36 Bennett, 2016.
37 Wilkinson and Pickett, 2009.
38 Smyth, 2016, p 286.

Chapter Two

1 Eliot, 1965.
2 Timmins, 2001, p 68.
3 McMillan, 1912.
4 Green, 1990, p 248.
5 Johnson, 1976.
6 Smith, 1785, p 305.
7 Ashurst and Venn, 2014, p 130.
8 Select Committee on the Poor Law Amendment Act, 1838, p 140.
9 Miller, 1992, p 2.
10 Lowe, 1867, pp 8, 10.
11 Ashurst and Venn, 2014.
12 Bolton, 2012.
13 Bourdieu and Passeron, 1979, pp 83–4.
14 Halsey et al, 1980.
15 Ibid, p 205.
16 Ford, 1969, p 37.
17 Douglas et al, 1971, p 51.
18 Ibid, p 53.
19 May, 2016.
20 Burgess et al, 2017.
21 Young, 2016.
22 Robbins Report, 1963.
23 Gurney-Dixon Report, 1954.
24 Douglas et al, 1971, p 190.
25 Jackson and Marsden, 1966, p 110.

26 Walkerdine, 1985, p 74.
27 Evans, 1991, pp 26–7.
28 Young, 1971.
29 Douglas et al, 1971, p 56.
30 The Parliamentary Secretary to the Ministry of Education (Mr Dennis Vosper), House of Commons Debates, 12 June 1956, vol 554, cols 534–46, *Hansard*.
31 Heaton, 1958, p 93.
32 Horrie, 2017, p 28.
33 Hunter, 1984.
34 Crosland, 1956, p 207.
35 Jones, 2003, p 78.
36 Ford, 1969.
37 Burgess, 1983, p 240.
38 Benn and Chitty, 1996.
39 Gewirtz et al, 1995, p 164.
40 Biressi and Nunn, 2013.
41 Ball, 2010, p 155.
42 Adams, 2015.
43 Brown, 1990, p 66.
44 Bourdieu, 1993, p 96.
45 Ibid.
46 OECD, 2009.
47 Jackson and Marsden, 1966, p 250.
48 Friedman et al, 2016.
49 Pells, 2016.
50 Braconier, 2012.
51 National Audit Office, 2017.
52 Allen, 2010.
53 Ferrari and Green, 2013.
54 Marsden, 1971.
55 Parkinson, 1970.
56 Stevenson, 2015, p 2.
57 Meek, 2016, p 8.
58 Johnson and Mansell, 2014, p 20.
59 Ibid, p 22.
60 House of Commons Education Committee, 2016, p 10.
61 Ibid, p 24.
62 Academies Commission, 2013, p 66.
63 Alegre and Ferrer, 2010.
64 Gorard, 2014.
65 Burns and Childs, 2016.
66 Gorard, 2016, p 143.
67 DfE, 2011.
68 NUT, 2013.
69 NAO, 2017.

70 OECD, 2013.
71 Burgess et al, 2015.
72 Poverty Site, 2015.
73 House of Commons Committee of Public Accounts, 2013.
74 Ibid, p 23.
75 DfE, 2014.
76 Guardian Datalab, 2012.
77 House of Commons Committee of Public Accounts, 2013.
78 DfE, 2015; Mansell, 2015.
79 National Audit Office, 2017.
80 Ibid, 2017, p 46.
81 Morton, 2016.
82 NUT/CPAG, 2017.
83 Gibbons et al, 2012.
84 RSA, 2015.

Chapter Three

1 Adonis, 2008.
2 Cameron, 2012.
3 Bailey and Ball, 2016, p 138.
4 Kulz, 2017.
5 Abraham, 2016, p 76.
6 Campbell, 2001.
7 Gove, 2014.
8 Taylor, 2015.
9 Ball et al, 2012.
10 Gillborn and Youdell, 2000.
11 Reay, 2012b.
12 Gerrard, 2013.
13 Dewey, 1916, p 325.
14 Tomlinson, 2005.
15 Wolf, 2002.
16 Hoskins et al, 2014.
17 Quoted in ibid, p 19.
18 Hartas, 2015.
19 Kalogrides and Loeb, 2013.
20 Massey and Fischer, 2006.
21 Crehan, 2016.
22 Clifton and Cook, 2012.

Chapter Four

1 Bourdieu and Champagne, 1999, p 423.
2 Savage, 2015.
3 Green, 1990.

4   Willis, 1977; Stahl, 2015.
5   Flanagan, BBC R4.
6   Parsons and Hallam, 2014.
7   Arnot and Reay, 2007.
8   Woolcock, 2008.
9   Reay and Wiliam, 1999.
10 Close et al, 1997, p 30.
11 Brown, 2016.
12 NUT, 2016.
13 Ibid, p 3.
14 Goffman, 1963.
15 Hall and Ozerk, 2008.
16 UNICEF, 2007.
17 Ipsos MORI, 2011.
18 The Children's Society, 2015, p 53.
19 Weale, 2017.
20 Hascher, 2011, p 102.

Chapter Five

1   Reay, 2013.
2   Reay, 2017a.
3   Jackson and Marsden, 1966, p 168.
4   Ibid, p 169.
5   Ibid, p 241.
6   Marsden, 1968, p 119.
7   'Melvin Bragg on Class and Culture', BBC documentary, 2012.
8   Bourdieu, 1999a, p 510.
9   Aitkenhead, 2014.
10 Walkerdine and Lucey, 1989.
11 Lawler, 2000, p 19.
12 Berlant, 2011, p 209.
13 Southgate et al, 2016, p 15.
14 Jackson and Marsden, 1966, p 183.
15 Wright Mills, 1943.
16 Moore and Claire, 2016, p 675.
17 Independent Commission on Fees, 2015.
18 Jerrim, 2013. The Russell Group of elite universities comprises: Birmingham, Bristol, Cambridge, Cardiff, Edinburgh, Glasgow, Imperial College of Science, Technology and Medicine, King's College London, Leeds, Liverpool, London School of Economics and Political Science, Manchester, Newcastle, Nottingham, Oxford, Sheffield, Southampton, University College London and Warwick. All are research-intensive universities.
19 Sutton Trust, 2010.
20 Boliver, 2013.
21 Jerrim, 2013.

22 Raffe and Croxford, 2013.
23 Elias and Purcell, 2012.
24 O'Carroll, 2016.
25 HESA, 2016.
26 Vignoles and Powdthavee, 2009.
27 Crawford et al, 2016, p 553.
28 Ali, 2016.
29 Reay et al, 2010.
30 Reay, 2006.
31 Bourdieu and Champagne, 1999, p 423.
32 Bathmaker et al, 2013.
33 Reay, 2017b.
34 Young, 1958.
35 Dorling, 2015.
36 Brown, 1990.
37 Fox, 1956, p 13.
38 Savage, 2015.
39 Brown, 1990; Gewirtz, 2001; Reay, 2013.
40 Stevenson and Clegg, 2011.
41 Crozier et al, 2008.
42 Tax Research blog, 2017.
43 Littler, 2017.
44 NUS, 2015.
45 Wilkinson and Pickett, 2009.
46 Britton et al, 2015.
47 Belfield et al, 2017.
48 HESA, 2017.
49 CIPD, 2015.
50 Coulson et al, 2017.
51 Britton et al, 2016.
52 Crawford et al, 2016.
53 Laurison and Friedman, 2016.
54 Britton et al, 2016.
55 DfE, 2016.

Chapter Six

1 Reay et al, 2005.
2 Bourdieu, 1990, p 108.
3 Woodward and Ward, 2000
4 Reay et al, 2011.
5 Kate, quoted in Reay et al, 2011.
6 Ford, 1969, p 129.
7 Savage, 2003, p 536.
8 Lareau, 2003.
9 Lucey and Reay, 2002.

[10] Russell, 2002.

[11] Kirby, 2016.

[12] Vincent et al, 2008.

[13] Reay, 2005; 2008.

[14] US, quoted in Fine et al, 2007, p 229.

[15] UK, quoted in Reay, 2006, p 297.

[16] Skeggs, 2004.

[17] Reay and Wiliam, 1999.

[18] Reay, 2006.

[19] Reay, 1998; Lareau, 2003.

[20] Sayer, 2005.

[21] Ryan, 2006, p 60.

[22] Sayer, 2005.

[23] Steedman, 1986.

[24] Coulson et al, 2017.

[25] Ibid, p 17.

[26] Arnot et al, 1999.

[27] Newitz and Wray, 1997.

[28] Archer and Francis, 2006.

[29] Leonardo, 2004.

Chapter Seven

[1] British Social Attitudes Survey, 2016.

[2] Reay, 2002.

[3] In Bourdieu and Wacquant, 1992, p 127.

[4] Hanley, 2016, p 17.

[5] Allen et al, 2012.

[6] Savage, 2000.

[7] Cassidy, 2001.

[8] Lucey and Reay, 2003; Reay and Lucey, 2004.

[9] Johnson, 1976.

[10] Brine, 2001.

[11] Reay, 2001.

[12] Bernstein, 1971, p 175.

[13] Freud, 1940.

[14] Layton, 2006, p 56.

[15] Savage et al, 2001.

[16] Stallybrass and White, 1986.

[17] Ibid, p 202.

Chapter Eight

[1] Jerrim, 2017.

[2] Gamsu, 2015.

[3] Miller et al, 2015; Castagné et al, 2016; Solis et al, 2016.

[4] Saltman, 2014, p 55.
[5] Corlett and Clarke, 2017.
[6] NUT, 2015.
[7] Evans and Tilley, 2017.
[8] ONS, 2017.
[9] Reay, 2012a.
[10] Quoted in Reay, 2012a, p 250.
[11] Gerrard, 2013, p 198.
[12] Eagleton, 1991, p 207.
[13] Smyth and Simmons, 2017.
[14] Adams, 2016.
[15] Antonucci, 2016.
[16] Ibid.
[17] OECD, 2015.
[18] EEF, 2016.
[19] Kulik and Kulik, 1982; 1984; Higgins et al, 2015.
[20] Crehan, 2016, p 248.
[21] Dunne et al, 2007.
[22] Cummings et al, 2012; Doyle and Griffin, 2012.
[23] Johnson et al, 1981; Kyndt et al, 2013.
[24] Crehan, 2016.
[25] McInerney, 2013.
[26] Ball et al, 1996; Reay, 2004.
[27] Burgess et al, 2006.
[28] Allen, 2007.
[29] Green et al, 2014.
[30] Reclaiming Schools, 2016.
[31] Mansell, 2011.
[32] Freire, 1970.
[33] Dewey, 1897.
[34] Ibid, p 79.
[35] hooks, 1994.
[36] Sewell, 2013, p 62.
[37] hooks, 2010.
[38] Martinez, 2016, p 280.
[39] Francis et al, 2017.
[40] Chakrabortty, 2017.
[41] Grasso et al, 2017.
[42] Varkey Foundation, 2017.
[43] Grasso et al, 2017.
[44] Taylor-Gooby, 2013, p 40.
[45] Taylor-Gooby, February 2017, personal communication.
[46] BSA, 2017.

Epilogue

[1] Jackson and Marsden, 1966, p 11.
[2] Bourdieu, in Bourdieu and Eagleton, 1992, p 117.
[3] Haylett, 2003, p 59.
[4] Kuhn, 1995, p 103.

References

Abraham, J. (2016) 'Schooling inequality: institutional practices and the reproduction of class inequalities in education', unpublished PhD thesis University of Cardiff.

Academies Commission (2013) *Unleashing greatness: Getting the best from an academised system*, London: Pearson with the Royal Society of Arts.

Adams, R. (2015) 'GCSE gap between rich and poor widens', *Guardian*, 29 January.

Adams, R. (2016) 'Latymer grammar school asks parents to make up financial shortfall', *Guardian*, 2 October.

Adonis, A. (2008) 'Academies and social mobility', speech to the National Academies Conference, www.standards.dfes.gov. uk/.../Andrew_Adonis_Speech_feb08.doc.

Aitkenhead, D. (2014) 'Steve McQueen: my hidden shame', *Guardian*, 4 January.

Alegre, A.M. and Ferrer, G. (2010) 'School regimes and education equity: some insights based on PISA 2006', *British Educational Research Journal*, vol 1, no 3, pp 433–61.

Ali, A. (2016) 'University grants for poorest students axed and replaced by loans', *Guardian*, 1 August.

Allen, R. (2007) 'Allocating pupils to their nearest secondary school: the consequences for social and ability stratification', *Urban Studies*, vol 44, no 4, pp 751–70.

Allen, R. (2010) 'Replicating Swedish "free school" reforms in England', *Research in Public Policy*, Summer, pp 4–7.

Allen, R., Burgess, S. and Mayo, J. (2012) 'The teacher labour market, teacher turnover and disadvantaged schools: new evidence for England', Working Paper No 12/294, Bristol: The Centre for Market and Public Organisation.

Antonucci, L. (2016) *Student lives in crisis: Deepening inequality in times of austerity*, Bristol: Policy Press.

Archer, L. and Francis, B. (2006) 'Challenging classes? Exploring the role of social class within the identities and achievement of British Chinese pupils', *Sociology*, vol 1, no 1, pp 29–49.

Arnot, M. and Reay, D. (2007) 'A sociology of pedagogic voice: power, inequality and transformation', *Discourse: Special Issue: Beyond 'Voice': New roles, relations, and contexts in researching with young people*, vol 28, no 3, pp 171–82.

Arnot, M., David, M. and Weiner, G. (1999) *Closing the gender gap*, Cambridge, England: Polity Press.

Ashurst, F. and Venn, C. (2014) *Inequality, poverty, education: A political economy of school exclusion*, London: Palgrave Macmillan.

Bailey, P. and Ball, S. (2016) 'The coalition government, the general election, and the policy rachet in education: a reflection on the "ghosts" of policy past, present and yet to come', in H. Bochel and M. Powell (eds) *The coalition government and social policy: Restructuring the welfare state*, Bristol: Policy Press, pp 125–49.

Ball, S. (2010) 'New class inequalities in education: why education policy may be looking in the wrong place! Education policy, civil society and social class', *International Journal of Sociology and Social Policy*, vol 30, no 3/4, pp 155–66.

Ball, S., Bowe, R. and Gewirtz, S. (1996) 'School choice, social class and distinction: the realization of social advantage in education', *Journal of Education Policy*, vol 1, no 1, pp 89–112.

Ball, S., Maguire, M., Braun, A., Perryman, J. and Hoskins, K. (2012) 'Assessment technologies in schools: deliverology and the play of dominations', *Research Papers in Education*, vol 27, no 5, pp 513–33.

Bathmaker, A.-M., Ingram, N. and Waller, R. (2013) 'Higher education, social class and the mobilisation of capitals: knowing and playing the game', *British Journal of Sociology of Education*, special issue on education and social mobility, vol 34, no 5/6, pp 723–43.

Belfield, C., Britton, J., Dearden, L. and van der Erve, L. (2017) *Higher education funding in England: Past, present and options for the future*, Briefing Note (BN211) for the Institute of Fiscal Studies, London: IFS.

Benn, C. and Chitty, C. (1996) *Thirty years on: Is comprehensive education alive and well or struggling to survive?*, London: David Fulton Publishers.

Bennett, A. (2016) *Keeping on keeping on*, London: Faber.

Bennett, J. (2012) 'Chav-spotting in Britain: the representation of social class as private choice', *Social Semiotics*, vol 1, no 1, 146–62.

Berlant, L. (2011) *Cruel optimism*, Durham, NC: Duke University Press.

Bernstein, B. (1970) 'Education cannot compensate for society', in C. Stoneman et al (eds) *Education for democracy*, London: Penguin Education Special, pp 110–21.

Bernstein, B. (1971) *Class, codes and control: Theoretical studies towards a sociology of language*, London: Routledge & Kegan Paul.

Beyond the Fringe (Acting Edition) (1964), Bennett, Alan, Dudley Moore, Peter Cook, Jonathan Miller, published by Samuel French, Inc.

Biressi, A. and Nunn, H. (2013) *Class and contemporary British culture*, London: Palgrave Macmillan.

Boliver, V. (2013) 'How fair is access to more prestigious UK universities?' *British Journal of Sociology*, vol 1, no 2, pp 344–64.

Bolton, P. (2012) *Education: Historical statistics*, London: House of Commons Briefing.

Bourdieu, P. (1990) *The logic of practice*, Cambridge: Polity Press.

Bourdieu, P. (1999a) 'The contradictions of inheritance', in P. Bourdieu et al, *Weight of the world: Social suffering in contemporary society*, Cambridge: Polity, pp 507–13.

Bourdieu, P. and Champagne, P. (1999) 'Outcasts on the inside', in P. Bourdieu et al, *Weight of the world: Social suffering in contemporary society*, pp 421–6, Cambridge: Polity.

Bourdieu, P. and Eagleton, T. (1992) 'Doxa and common life', *New Left Review* 1/191, January–February, pp 111-21.

Bourdieu, P. and Passeron, J.-C. (1979) *The inheritors: The French students and their relation to culture*, trans R. Nice, Chicago and London: The University of Chicago Press.

Bourdieu, P. and Wacquant, L. (1992) *An invitation to reflexive sociology*, Chicago: University of Chicago Press.

Braconier, H. (2012) 'Reforming education in England', OECD Economics Department Working Papers No 939, Paris: OECD Publishing.

Bradley, H. (1996) *Fractured identities: Changing patterns of inequality*, Cambridge: Cambridge University Press.

Brine, J. (2001) 'Education, social exclusion and the supranational state', International Journal of Inclusive Education, vol 5, no 2/3, pp 119–31.

British Social Attitudes Survey (2016) *33rd Annual British Social Attitudes Report*, London: NatCen.

British Social Attitudes Survey (2017) *British Social Attitudes Report 34: A kind-hearted but not soft-hearted country*, London: National Centre for Social Research.

Britton, J., Crawford, C. and Dearden, L. (2015) 'Analysis of the higher education funding reforms announced in summer budget 2015', IFS Briefing Note BN 174, London: The Institute for Fiscal Studies, July 2015.

Britton, J., Dearden, L., Shephard, N. and Vignoles, A. (2016) 'How English domiciled graduate earnings vary with gender, institution attended, subject and socio-economic background', IFS Working Paper (W16/06), London: The Institute for Fiscal Studies.

Brown, P. (1990) 'The "third wave": education and the ideology of parentocracy', *British Journal of Sociology of Education*, vol 1, no 1, pp 65–85.

Brown, R. (2012) 'Figures reveal deep inequalities between rich and poor universities. The gap in income and resources between universities is even greater than that between public and state schools', *Guardian*, 24 September.

Brown, Z. (2016) 'Dear Nicky Morgan', *The New Statesman* 27 May .

Burgess, R. (1983) *Experiencing comprehensive education*, London: Methuen.

Burgess, S., Briggs, A., McConnell, B., Slater, H. (2006) 'School choice in England: background facts', CMPO Working Paper Series no 06/159, Institute of Public Affairs, University of Bristol.

Burn, K. and Childs, A. (2016) 'Responding to poverty through education and teacher education initiatives: a critical evaluation of key trends in government policy in England 1997–2015', *Journal of Education for Teaching*, vol 42, no 4, pp 387–403.

Cameron, D. (2012) Speech to the Scottish Conservatives, Dumfries, http://www.scottishconservatives.com/2012/04/david-cameron-speechto-scottish-conservative-in-dumfries/, accessed 9 May 2017.

Campbell, A. (2001) 'The day of the bog-standard comprehensive is over', speech, Labour party Spring Conference, February, Glasgow.

Cassidy, S. (2001) 'Report insists comprehensives "are not a failed experiment"', *The Independent*, 19 July.

Castagné, R.R. et al (2016) 'A life course approach to explore the biological embedding of socioeconomic position and social mobility through circulating inflammatory markers', *Scientific Reports*, vol 6, p 25170.

Chakrabortty, A. (2017) 'We need the state now more than ever. But our belief in it has gone', *Guardian*, 1 February.

CIPD (Chartered Institute of Personnel and Development (2015) *Over-qualification and skills mismatch in the graduate labour market*, London: CIPD.

Clarke, S. and D'Arcy, C. (2016) *Low pay Britain 2016*, London: The Resolution Foundation.

Clifton, J. and Cook, W. (2012) *A long division: Closing the attainment gap in England's secondary schools*, London: IPPR.

Close, G.S, Furlong, T. and Simon, S.A. (1997) *The validity of the 1996 Key Stage 2 tests in English, mathematics and science*, Report prepared for Association of Teachers and Lecturers (London,King's College London School of Education).

Coren, G. (2016) 'Eating out: restaurant review of Wazan', *The Times Magazine*, 17 September, p 105.

Corlett, A. and Clarke, S. (2017) *Living standards 2017: The past, present and possible future of UK incomes*, London: The Resolution Foundation.

Coulson, S., Garforth, L., Payne, G. and Wastell, E. (2017) 'Admissions, adaptations and anxieties: social class inside and outside the elite university', in R. Waller, N. Ingram and M. Ward (eds) *Degrees of injustice: Social class inequalities in university admissions, experiences and outcomes*, Abingdon: Routledge.

Crawford, C., Gregg, P., Macmillan, L., Vignoles, A. and Wyness, G. (2016) 'Higher education, career opportunities, and intergenerational inequality', *Oxford Review of Economic Policy*, vol 32, no 4, pp 553–75.

Crehan, L. (2016) *Cleverlands: The secrets behind the success of the world's educational superpowers*, London: Unbound.

Crosland, C.A.R. (1956) *The future of socialism*, London: Cape.

Crozier, G., Reay, D. and Clayton, J. (2008) 'Different strokes for different folks: diverse students in diverse institutions', *Research papers in Education*, vol 1, no 2, pp 167–77.

Cummings, C., Laing, K., Law, J., McLaughlin, J., Papps, I., Todd, L. and Woolner, P. (2012) *Can changing aspirations and attitudes impact on educational attainment?* York: Joseph Rowntree Foundation.

Dewey, J. (1897) 'My pedagogic creed', *The School Journal*, vol 54, no 3, pp 77–80.

Dewey, J. (1916) *Democracy and education*, New York: The Free Press.

DfE (Department for Education) (2014) *Statistical first release income and expenditure in academies in England*, 2 October, London: DfE.

DfE (2015) 'Prime Minister announces landmark wave of free schools', press release, 9 March.

DfE (2016) *Employment and earnings outcomes of higher education graduates: Experimental data from the longitudinal education outcomes (LEO) dataset*, London: DfE.

DfE (2017) *Analysing family circumstances and education: A technical consultation document*, April, London: DfE.

Dorling, D. (2015) *Injustice: Why social inequality still persists*, Bristol: Policy Press.

Douglas, J., Ross, J. and Simpson, H. (1971) *All our Futures*, London: Panther Books Ltd.

Doyle, M. and Griffin, M. (2012) 'Raised aspirations and attainment? A review of the impact of Aimhigher (2004–2011) on widening participation in higher education in England', *London Review of Education*, vol 1, no 1, pp 75–88.

Dunne, M., Humphreys, S., Sebba, J., Dyson, A., Gallannaugh, F., Muijs, D., Department for Children, Schools and Families (DCSF) (2007) *Effective teaching and learning for pupils in low attaining groups,* research report, London: Department for Children Schools and Families.

Eagleton, T. (1991) *Ideology: An introduction*, London: Verso.

EEF (Education Endowment Foundation) (2016) Education Endowment Foundation Teaching and Learning Toolkit, https://educationendowmentfoundation.org.uk/resources/teaching-learning-toolkit, accessed 3 December 2016.

Elias, P. and Purcell, K. (2012) 'Higher education and social background', in Institute for Social and Economic Research (ed) *Understanding Society Findings*,Colchester: Institute for Social and Economic Research, University of Essex, pp 23–4.

Eliot, T.S. (1965) 'The aims of education', in *To criticize the critic and other writings*, Nebraska: University of Nebraska Press, pp 61-124.

Elliott, L. (2016) 'A zero-hours contract is not "flexibility" but exploitation – and it's rising', *Guardian*, 9 March.

Evan, M. (1991) *A good school: Life at a girls' grammar school in the 1950s*, London: The Women's Press.

Evans, G. and Tilley, J. (2017) *The new class war: The political and social marginalization of the British working class*, Oxford: Oxford University Press.

Ferrari, E. and Green, M. (2013) 'Travel to school and housing markets: a case study of Sheffield, England', *Environment and Planning A*, vol 45, no 11, pp 2771–88.

Fine, M., Burns, A., Torre, M. and Payne, Y. (2007) 'How class matters: the geography of educational desire and despair in schools and courts', in L. Weis (ed) *The way class works*, New York: Routledge.

Ford, J. (1969) *Social class and the comprehensive school*, London: Routledge & Kegan Paul.

Foster, D. (2015) 'Free schools', *London Review of Books*, vol 1, no 9, pp 8–9.

Fox, A. (1956) 'Class and equality', *Social Commentary* May, pp 11–13.

Francis, B., Archer, L., Hodgen, J., Pepper, D., Taylor, B. and Travers, M. (2017) 'Exploring the relative lack of impact of research on "ability grouping" in England: a discourse analytic account', *Cambridge Journal of Education*, vol 47, no 1, pp 1-17.

Freire, P. (1970) *Pedagogy of the oppressed*, New York, Continuum.

Freud, S. (1940) *An outline of psychoanalysis*, New York: W.W. Norton & Co.

Friedman, S., O'Brien, D. and Laurison, D. (2016) '"Like skydiving without a parachute": how class origin shapes occupational trajectories in British acting', *Sociology*, doi: 10.1177/0038038516629917.

Gamsu, S. (2015) 'The logic of the ladder – elite widening participation and the implicit "scholarship boy" discourse which never went away', https://solgamsu.wordpress. com/2015/06/16/the-logic-of-the-ladder-elite-widening-participation-and-the-implicit-scholarship-boy-discourse-which-never-went-away/.

Gerrard, J. (2013) 'Class analysis and the emancipatory potential of education', *Educational Theory*, vol 13, no 2, pp 185–201.

Gewirtz, S. (2001) 'Cloning the Blairs: New Labour's programme for the re-socialization of working-class parents', *Journal of Education Policy*, vol 16, no 4, pp 365–78.

Gewirtz, S., Ball, S. and Bowe, R. (1995) *Markets, choice and equity in education*, Buckingham: Open University Press.

Gibbons, S., McNally, S. and Viarengo, M. (2012) *Does additional spending help urban schools? An evaluation using discontinuities*, Centre for the Study of the Economics of Education Discussion Paper No 128, http://cee.lse.ac.uk/ceedps/ceedp128.pdf.

Gillborn, D. and Youdell, P. (2000) *Rationing education*, Buckingham: Open University Press.

Goffman, S. *(1963) Stigma: Notes on the management of spoiled identity*, New Jersey: Prentice Hall.

Gorard, S. (2014) 'The link between academies in England, pupil outcomes and local patterns of socio-economic segregation between schools', *Research Papers in Education*, vol 1, no 3, 268–84.

Gorard, S. (2016) 'The complex determinants of school intake characteristics and segregation, England 1989 to 2014', *Cambridge Journal of Education*, vol 1, no 1, pp 131–46.

Grasso, M., Farrall, S. and Gray, E. et al (2017) 'Thatcher's children, Blair's babies, political socialisation and trickle-down value-change: An age, period and cohort analysis', *British Journal of Political Science*, https://doi.org/10.1017/S0007123416000375.

Green, A. (1990) *Education and state formation: The rise of education systems in England, France and the USA*, Basingstoke: Macmillan.

Green, F., Allen, R. and Jenkins, A. (2014) 'Research briefing summary: the social composition of free schools after three years', http://www.llakes.org/wp-content/uploads/2014/08/Free-Schools-briefing-document.pdf.

Guardian Datalab (2012) 'Education in, London: pupils by race, poverty and language for every local authority What kinds of children attend London's state schools? See how key education indicators differ by local authority'.

Gurney-Dixon Report (1954) *Early leaving: A report of the Central Advisory Council for Education (England)*, London: Her Majesty's Stationery Office.

Hall, K. and Øzerk, K. (2008) *Primary curriculum and assessment: England and other countries*, Primary Review Research Survey 3/1, Cambridge: University of Cambridge Faculty of Education.

Halsey, A.H, Heath, A.F. and Ridge, J.M. (1980) *Origins and destinations: Family, class, and education in modern Britain*. Oxford: Clarendon Press.

Hanley, L. (2016) *Respectable: The experience of class*, London: Allen Lane.

Hartas, D. (2015) 'Parenting for social mobility? Home learning, parental warmth, class and educational outcomes', *Journal of Education Policy*, vol 1, no 1, pp 21–38.

Hascher, T. (2011) 'Wellbeing', in S. Jarvela (ed) *Social and emotional aspects of learning*, London: Academic Press, pp 99–112.

Haylett, C. (2003) 'Culture, class and urban policy: reconsidering equality', *Antipode*, vol 35, no 1, pp 55–73.

Heath, O. (2016) 'Policy alienation, social alienation and working-class abstention in Britain, 1964–2010', *British Journal of Political Science*, DOI: https://doi.org/10.1017/S0007123416000272, pp 1–21.

Heaton, P.R. (1958) 'External examinations in the secondary modern school', in G.B. Jeffery (ed) *External examinations in secondary schools: Their place and function*, London: Harrap, pp 93–94.

HESA (Higher Education Statistics Agency) (2016) 'Student data 2015–2016', https://www.hesa.ac.uk/files/UKPIs_2015–16_Experimental.xlsx.

HESA (2017) 'Destinations of leavers from higher education in the United Kingdom for the academic year 2015/16', Statistical First Release SFR245 , https://www.hesa.ac.uk/news/29-06-2017/sfr245-destinations-of-leavers

Higgins, S., Katsipataki, M., Coleman, R., Henderson, P., Major, L., Coe, R. and Mason, D. (2015) *The trust – education endowment foundation teaching and learning toolkit*, London: Education Endowment Foundation.

HMRC (Her Majesty's Revenue and Customs) (2016) 'Largest ever list of national minimum wage offenders published', https://www.gov.uk/government/news/largest-ever-list-of-national-minimum-wage-offenders-published, accessed 29 August 2016.

hooks, b. (1984) *Feminist theory from margin to center*, Boston, MA: South End Press.

hooks, b. (2010) *Teaching critical thinking: Practical wisdom*, New York: Routledge.

Horrie, C. (2017) 'Back to the old days?' *Guardian*, 4 May, pp 27–29.

Hoskins, B., Janmaat, J., Han, C. and Muijs, D. (2014) 'Inequalities in the education system and the reproduction of socioeconomic disparities in voting in England, Denmark and Germany: the influence of country context, tracking and self-efficacy on voting intentions of students age 16–18', *Compare*, vol 1, no 5, pp 801–25.

House of Commons Business, Innovation and Skills Committee (2016a) *Employment practices at Sports Direct: Third Report of Session 2016–17*, London: House of Commons.

House of Commons Business, Innovation and Skills Committee (2016b) *Oral evidence: Working practices at Sports Direct*, Third Report of Session 2016–17, London: House of Commons.

House of Commons Committee of Public Accounts (2013) *Managing the expansion of the Academies Programme: Forty-first Report of Session 2012–13,* London: House of Commons.

House of Commons Education Committee (2014) *Underachievement in education of white working class children: First Report of Session 2014–15*, London: House of Commons.

House of Commons Education Committee (2016) *Multi academy trusts: Seventh Report of Session 2016–17*, London: House of Commons.

Hunter, C. (1984) 'The political devaluation of comprehensives: what of the future?' in S.J. Ball (ed) *Comprehensive schooling: A reader*, Lewes: Falmer Press, pp 273–92.

Independent Commission on Fees (2015) *Final report*, London: The Sutton Trust.

Ipsos MORI (2011) *Children's well-being in UK, Sweden and Spain: The role of inequality and materialism*, London Ipsos–MORI social Research Institute.

Jackson, B. and Marsden, D. (1966) *Education and the working class*, London: Penguin Books.

Jacques, M. (2016) 'The death of neoliberalism and the crisis in western politics', *Observer* 21 August, pp 31–3.

Jensen, T. (2013) '"Mumsnetiquette": online affect within parenting culture', in C. Maxwell and p Aggleton (eds) *Privilege, agency and affect: Understanding the production and effects of action*, Basingstoke,: Palgrave Macmillan. pp 127–45.

Jerrim, J. (2013) *Family background and access to high 'status' universities*, London: The Sutton Trust.

Jerrim, J. (2017) *Global gaps: Comparing socio-economic gaps in the performance of highly able UK pupils internationally*, London: The Sutton Trust.

Johnson, D.W., Maruyama, G., Johnson, R. and Nelson, D. (1981) 'Effects of cooperative, competitive and individualistic goal structures on achievement: a meta-analysis', *Psychological Bulletin*, vol 89, no 1, pp 47–62.

Johnson, M. and Mansell, W. (2014) *Education not for sale: A TUC research report*, London: Trades Union Congress.

Johnson, R. (1976) 'Notes on the schooling of the English working class 1780–1850', in R. Dale et al (eds) *Schooling and capitalism: A sociological reader*, Milton Keynes: Open University Press.

Jones, K. (2003) *Education in Britain: 1944 to the present*, Cambridge: Polity Press.

Jones, O. (2011) *Chavs: The demonization of the working class*, London: Verso Books.

Jones, O. (2016) 'The left must refocus on class, and show it still cares about workers', *Guardian*, 18 August, p 35.

JRF (Joseph Rowntree Foundation) (2016) *UK poverty: Causes, costs and solutions*, York: JRF.

Kalogrides, D. and Loeb, S. (2013) 'Different teachers, different peers', *Educational Researcher*, vol 42, pp 304–16.

Kirby, P. (2016) *Shadow schooling: Private tuition and social mobility in the UK*, London: The Sutton Trust.

Kuhn, A. (1995) *Family secrets: Acts of memory and imagination*, London: Verso.

Kulik, C. and Kulik, A. (1982) 'Effects of ability grouping on secondary school pupils: a meta-analysis of evaluation findings', *American Educational Research Journal*, vol 1, no 3, pp 415–28.

Kulik, C. and Kulik, A. (1984) 'Effects of ability grouping on elementary school pupils: a meta-analysis', Annual Meeting of the American Psychological Association.

Kulz, C. (2017) 'Heroic heads, mobility mythologies and the power of ambiguity', *British Journal of Sociology of Education*, vol 1, no 2, pp 85–104.

Kynaston, D. (2009) *Family Britain, 1951–57*, London: Bloomsbury.

Kyndt, E., Raes, E., Lismont, B., Timmers, F., Dochy, F. and Cascallar, E. (2013) 'A meta-analysis of the effects of face-to-face cooperative learning. Do recent studies falsify or verify earlier findings?', *Educational Research Review*, vol 10, pp 133–49.

Lansley, S. and Reed, H. (2013) *How to boost the wage share*, London: TUC.

Lareau, A. (2003) *Unequal childhoods*, Los Angeles: University of California Press.

Laurison, D. and Friedman, S. (2016) 'The class pay gap in higher professional and managerial occupations', *American Sociological Review*, vol 81, no 4, pp 668–95.

Lawler, S. (2000) *Mothering the self: Mothers, daughters, subjects*, London: Routledge.

Lawler, S. (2014) 'Heroic workers and angry young men: nostalgic stories of class in England', *European Journal of Cultural Studies*, vol 17, no 6, pp 701–20.

Layton, L. (2006) 'That place gives me the heebie jeebies', in L. Layton, N. Hollander and S. Gutwill (eds) *Psychoanalysis, class and politics: Encounters in the clinical setting*, New York: Routledge, pp 51–64.

Leonardo, Z. (2004) 'The souls of white folks', in D. Gillborn and G. Ladson-Billings (eds) *Multicultural education*, London and New York: Routledge Falmer.

Littler, J. (2017) *Against meritocracy: Culture, power and myths of mobility*, London: Routledge

Lowe, R. (1867) 'Primary and classical education', in B. Simon (1960) *Studies in the history of education 1780–1870*, London, Lawrence and Wishart.

Lucey, H. and Reay, D. (2002) 'Carrying the beacon of excellence: pupil performance, gender and social class', *Journal of Education Policy*, vol 17, no 3, pp 321–36.

Lucey, H. and Reay, D. (2003) 'A market in waste: psychic and structural dimensions of school-choice policy in the UK and children's narratives on "demonized" schools', *Discourse*, vol 23, no 2, pp 253–66.

Mani, A., Mullainathan, S., Shafi, E. and Zhao, J. (2013) 'Poverty impedes cognitive function', *Science, vol* 341, no 6149, pp 976–80.

Mansell, W. (2011) 'Co-operative schools: the antidote to academies', *Guardian*, 15 August.

Mansell, W. (2015) 'The 60% extra funds enjoyed by England's free school pupils', *Guardian*, 25 August.

Marsden, D. (1968) 'Dennis Marsden' in R. Goldman (ed) *Breakthrough: Autobiographical accounts of the education of some socially disadvantaged children*, London: Routledge, pp 106–23.

Martinez, R. (2016) *Creating freedom: Power, control and the fight for our freedom*, London: Canongate.

Massey, D. and Fischer, M. (2006) 'The effect of childhood segregation on minority academic performance at selective colleges', *Ethnic and Racial Studies*, vol 1, no 1, pp 1–26.

May, T. (2016) 'Britain, the great meritocracy: Prime Minister's speech', speech delivered in London, 9 September. .

McInerney, L. (2013) 'Gove's "progressive betrayal" seems to be a private school phenomenon', *Guardian*, 17 December.

McMillan, M. (1912) 'How I became a socialist', *Labour Leader*, 11 July.

Micky Flanagan BBC Radio 4 Extra - Micky Flanagan: What Chance Change?, 1970s 25th May 2010

Miller, G., Tianyi , Y., Chen, E. and Brody, G. (2015) 'Self-control forecasts better psychosocial outcomes but faster epigenetic aging in low-SES youth', www.pnas.org/cgi/doi/10.1073/pnas.1505063112, accessed 17 July 2016.

Miller, J. (1992) *More has meant women: The feminisation of schooling*, London: Tufnell Park Press with the Institute of Education.

Moore, A and Claire, M (2016) '"Cruel optimism": Teacher attachment to professionalism in an era of performativity', *Journal of Education Policy*, vol 31, no 1, pp 666-77.

Morton, K. (2016) 'Disadvantaged children will be hardest hit by school funding changes', *Nursery World*, 4 November, http://www.nurseryworld.co.uk/nursery-world/news/1159421/disadvantaged-children-will-be-hardest-hit-by-school-funding-changes.

NAO (National Audit Office) (2017) *Capital funding for schools*, London: Department for Education.

Newitz, A. and Wray, M. (1997) *White trash: Race and class in America* New York: Routledge.

NUS (National Union of Students (2013) *Mental Distress Survey Overview*, London: NUS Services Limited, https://www.nus.org.uk/en/news/20-per-cent-of-students-consider-themselves-to-have-a-mental-health-problem/.

NUT (National Union of Teachers) (2013) 'Free schools – free for all?', www.teachers.org.uk/sites/default/files2014/free-schools-16pp-a4-8963_0.pdf.

NUT (2015) 'Supply teachers' anger at agency rip off', press release, 28 October, https://www.teachers.org.uk/news-events/press-releases-england/supply-teachers-anger-agency-rip.

NUT (2016) 'The crisis in primary assessment: report of an NUT Survey of primary teachers and head teachers', https://www.teachers.org.uk/news-events/press.../crisis-primary-assessment-nut-survey.

NUT/CPAG (2017) 'NUT/CPAG figures show government school funding proposals will hit schools with the poorest children hardest', https://www.teachers.org.uk/news-events/press-releases-england/nut-cpag-figures-show-poorest-children-hit-hardest, accessed 3 March 2017.

O'Carroll, L. (2016) 'Percentage of poorer students accepted to Oxbridge falls, figures show', *Guardian*, 18 February.

OECD (2010) *PISA 2009 at a Glance*, OECD Publishing, http://dx.doi.org/10.1787/9789264095298-en.

OECD (2013) 'Are countries moving towards more equitable education systems?' PISA in Focus No 25, 2013/02 (February), http://www.oecd.org/pisa/pisainfocus/pisa%20in%20 focus%20n25%20(eng)--FINAL.pdf, accessed 5 September 2016.

OECD (2015) *In it together: Why less inequality benefits all*, Paris: OECD.

ONS (2017) *Statistical bulletin: UK labour market: Estimates of employment, unemployment, economic inactivity and other employment-related statistics for the UK. August 2017*, London: Office for National Statistics.

Parkinson, M. (1970) *The Labour Party and the organisation of secondary education, 1918–1965*, London: Routledge.

Parsons, S. and Hallam, S. (2014) 'The impact of streaming on attainment at age seven: evidence from the Millennium Cohort Study', *Oxford Review of Education*, vol 40, no 5, pp 567–89.

Pells, R. (2016) 'Private school students have a better chance of being Olympic champions, claims Sir Steve Redgrave', *Independent*.

Poverty Site (2015) 'Concentrations of poor children', http:www. poverty.org.uk/19/index/shtml, accessed August 2016.

Raffe, D. and Croxford, L. (2013) 'How stable is the stratification of higher education in England and Scotland?' *British Journal of Sociology of Education*, vol 1, no 2, pp 313–35.

Reay, D. (1998) *Class work: Mothers' involvement in children's schooling*, London: University College Press.

Reay, D. (2001) 'Finding or losing yourself? Working class relationships to education', *Journal of Education Policy*, vol 1, no 4, pp 333–46.

Reay, D. (2002) 'Shaun's story: troubling discourses of white working class masculinities', *Gender and Education*, vol 1, no 3, pp 221–34.

Reay, D. (2004) '"Mostly roughs and toughs": Social class, race and representation in inner city schooling', *Sociology*, vol 38, no 4, pp 1005-23.

Reay, D. (2005) 'Beyond consciousness? The psychic landscape of social class', *Sociology*, Special issue on 'Social Class', vol 39, no 5, pp 911-28.

Reay, D. (2006) 'The zombie stalking English schools: social class and educational inequality', *British Journal of Educational Studies*, Special issue on Social Justice, vol 54, no 3, pp 288–307.

Reay, D. (2008) 'Psycho-social aspects of white middle-class identities: Desiring and defending against the class and ethnic "other" in urban multiethnic schooling', *Sociology*, vol 42, no 6, pp 1072–88.

Reay, D. (2012a) 'What would a socially just education system look like? Saving the minnows from the pike', *Journal of Education Policy*, Special issue on Socially Just Education, vol 27, no 5, pp 587–99.

Reay, D. (2012b) '"We never get a fair chance": working class experiences of education in the twenty-first century', in W. Atkinson, S. Roberts and M. Savage (eds) *Class inequality in Austerity Britain*, Basingstoke: Palgrave Macmillan.

Reay, D. (2013) 'Social mobility, a panacea for austere times : tales of emperors, frogs, and tadpoles', *British Journal of Sociology of Education*, Special Issue on Social Mobility, vol 34, no 5/6, pp 660–77.

Reay, D. (2017a) 'The cruelty of social mobility: individual success at the cost of collective failure', in S. Lawler and G. Payne (eds) *Everyone a winner? Social mobility in the 21st century*, Abingdon: Routledge.

Reay, D. (2017b) 'A tale of two universities: class work in the field of higher education', in R. Waller, N. Ingram and M. Ward (eds) *Degrees of injustice: Social class inequalities in university admissions, experiences and outcomes*, Abingdon: Routledge.

Reay, D. and Lucey, H. (2004) 'Stigmatised choices: social class, social exclusion and secondary school markets in the inner city', *Pedagogy, Culture and Society*, vol 1, no 1, pp 35–51.

Reay, D. and Wiliam, D. (1999) '"I'll be a nothing": structure, agency and the construction of identity through assessment', *British Educational Research Journal*, vol 1, no 3, pp 343–54.

Reay, D., Crozier, G. and Clayton, J. (2010) '"Fitting in" or "standing out": working-class students in UK higher education', *British Educational Research Journal*, vol 1, no 1, pp 107–24.

Reay, D., Crozier, G. and James, D. (2011) *White middle class identities and urban schooling*, Basingstoke: Palgrave.

Reay, D., David, M.E. and Ball, S. (2005) *Degrees of choice: Social class, race and gender in higher education*, Trentham Books.

Reclaiming Schools (2016), https://reclaimingschools. org/2016/11/03/children-are-more-than-a-score/.

Resolution Foundation (2012) *Gaining from growth: The final report of the Commission on Living Standards*, London: The Resolution Foundation.

Robbins Report (1963) *Higher Education Report of the Committee appointed by the Prime Minister under the Chairmanship of Lord Robbins*, London: Her Majesty's Stationery Office.

Robinson, C. and Fielding, M. (2007) 'Children and their primary schools: pupils' voices', Primary Review Research Survey 5/3, Cambridge: University of Cambridge Faculty of Education.

Russell, J. (2002) 'Pay as you learn', *Guardian*, 8 April.

Ryan, F. (2016) 'We can eradicate poverty, if we choose to', *Guardian*, 6 September, p 29.

Ryan, J. (2006) 'Class is in you: an exploration of some social class issues in psychotherapeutic work', *British Journal of Psychotherapy*, vol 1, no 1, pp 49–62.

Saltman, K.J. (2014) 'The austerity school: grit, character, and the privatization of public education', *Symploke*, vol 22, no 1/2, pp 41–57.

Savage, M. (2000) *Class analysis and social transformation*, Milton Keynes: Open University Press.

Savage, M. (2003) 'A new class paradigm?' review article, *British Journal of Sociology of Education*, vol 1, no 4, pp 535–41.

Savage, M. (2015) *Social class in the 21st century*, London: Penguin Books.

Savage, M., Bagnall, G. and Longhurst, B. (2001) 'Ordinary, ambivalent and defensive: class identities in the Northwest of England', *Sociology*, vol 1, no 4, pp 875–92.

Sayer, A. (2005) *The moral significance of class*, Cambridge: Cambridge University Press.

Select Committee on the Poor Law Amendment Act (1938) Report from the Select Committee on the Poor Law Amendment Act with the minutes of evidence, London: House of Commons.

Sewell, J. (2013) 'bell hooks on critical thinking: the successes and limitations of practical wisdom', PhD thesis, Canada: University of Windsor.

Sibieta, L. (2015) *Schools spending*, London: Institute of Fiscal Studies with The Nuffield Foundation.

Skeggs, B. (2004) *Class, self, culture*, London: Routledge.

Smith, A. (1785) *An inquiry into the nature and causes of the wealth of nations*, London, Liberty Press.

Smyth, J. (2016) '"Education and the working class": a conversation with the work of Dennis Marsden and his contribution to the sociology of education', *Journal of Educational Administration and History*, vol 48, no 4, pp 275–89.

Smyth, J. and Simmons, P. (2017) 'Where is class in the analysis of working class education?' in J. Smyth and P. Simmons (eds) *Education and working class youth*, London: Palgrave Macmillan, pp 1–19.

Solis, B., Fantin, R., Kelly-Irving, M. and Delpierre, C. (2016) 'Physiological wear-and-tear and later subjective health in mid-life: Findings from the 1958 British birth cohort', *Psychoneuroendocrinology*, vol 74, pp 24–33.

Southgate, E., Brosnan, C., Lempp, H., Kelly, B., Wright, S., Outram, S. and Bennett, A. (2016) 'Travels in extreme social mobility: how first-in-family students find their way into and through medical education', *Critical Studies in Education*, http://dx.doi.org/10.1080/17508487.2016.1263223.

Stahl, G. (2015) *Identity, neoliberalism and aspiration: Educating white working-class boys*, London: Routledge.

Stallybrass, P. and White, A. (1986) *The politics and poetics of transgression* London, Routledge.

Steedman, C. (1986) *Landscape for a good woman: A story of two lives*, London: Virago.

Stevenson, J. and Clegg, S. (2011) 'Possible selves: students orientating themselves towards the future through extracurricular activity' *British Educational Research Journal,* vol 37, no 2, pp 231–46.

Sutton Trust (2010) 'Private students 55 times more likely to go to Oxbridge than poor students', press release, 22 December, http://www.suttontrust.com/newsarchive/private-school-pupils-55-times-likely-go-oxbridge-poor-students/, accessed 12 April 2017.

Taylor, R. (2015) 'Students in deprived neighbourhoods being denied access to "tough subjects", London: RSA, 11 February, https://www.thersa.org/about-us/media/2015/students-in-deprived-neighbourhoods-being-denied-access-to-tough-subjects, accessed 20 April 2017.

Taylor-Gooby, P. (2013) 'Why do people stigmatise the poor at a time of rapidly increasing inequality, and what can be done about it?', *The Political Quarterly*, vol 84, no 1, pp 31-42.

Taylor-Gooby, P., Leruth, B. and Chung, H. (2015) 'Where next for the UK welfare state? Austerity, policy responses and public attitudes', Paper presented at the 2015 annual ESPAnet Conference, Odense, 4 September.

The Children's Society (2015) *The good childhood report*, London: The Children's Society.

Todd, S. (2014) *The people: The rise and fall of the working class 1910–2010*, London: John Murray.

Tomlinson, S. (2005) *Education in a post-welfare society*, 2nd edn, Maidenhead: Open University Press.

Trading Economics (2016) http://www.tradingeconomics.com/united-kingdom/unemployment-rate, accessed 11 September 2016.

Tyler, I. (2008) 'Chav mum chav scum: class disgust in contemporary Britain', *Feminist Media Studies*, vol 1, no 1, 17–34.

Tyler, I. and Bennett, B. (2010) '"Celebrity chav": fame, femininity and social class', *European Journal of Cultural Studies*, vol 1, no 3, 375–93.

UNICEF (2007) 'Child poverty in perspective: an overview of child well-being in rich countries', Innocenti Report Card 7, Innocenti Research Centre, Florence: UNICEF.

Varkey Foundation (2017) *What the world's young people think and feel: Global young people report*, London: The Varkey Foundation.

Varsity (2009) 'Wealth survey', issue 687, 23 January, p 4.

Vignoles, A.F. and Powdthavee, N. (2009) 'The socioeconomic gap in university dropouts', *B.E. Journal of Economic Analysis and Policy*, vol 9, pp 1–36.

Vincent, C., Ball, S. and Braun, A. (2008) 'Childcare and social class: caring for young children in the UK', *Critical Social Policy*, vol 28 no 1, pp 5–26.

Walker, P. (2016) 'Warnings over abolition of child poverty unit', *Guardian*, 20 December, p 4.

Walkerdine, V. (1985) 'Dreams from an ordinary childhood', in L. Heron (ed) *Truth, dare or promise: Girls growing up in the fifties*, London: Virago, pp 63–78.

Walkerdine, V. and Lucey, H. (1989) *Democracy in the kitchen: Regulating mothers and socialising daughters*, London: Virago.

Weale, S. (2017) 'UK second only to Japan for young people's poor mental wellbeing', *Guardian*, 8 February.

Wilkinson, R. and Pickett, K. (2009) *The spirit level: Why equal societies almost always do better*, London and New York: Allen Lane.

Willis, P. (1977) *Learning to labour*, Farnborough: Saxon House.

Wolf, A. (2002) *Does education matter?* London: Penguin Books.

Woodward, W. and Ward, L. (2000) Elitism row fuelled by study into university admissions, *The Guardian*, Monday 5 June.

Woolcock, N. (2008) 'English children "are most tested in the world"', *The Times*, 8 February.

Wright Mills, C. (1943) 'The professional ideology of social pathologists', *American Journal of Sociology*, vol 1, no 2, pp 165–80.

Young, L. (2016) 'If Theresa May wants to bring back grammar schools, she is no champion of social mobility', *Independent*, 7 August.

Young, M. (1958) *The rise of the meritocracy*, London: Thames & Hudson.

Index